CRY IN THE WILDERNESS
"Hear ye the voice of the Lord"

By TAY THOMAS

*Issued under the auspices of the
Alaska Council of Churches*

WIPF & STOCK · Eugene, Oregon

Wipf and Stock Publishers
199 W 8th Ave, Suite 3
Eugene, OR 97401

Cry in the Wilderness
"Hear ye the voice of the Lord"
By Thomas, Tay
Copyright©1967 by Thomas, Tay
ISBN 13: 978-1-61097-037-2
Publication date 5/4/2011
Previously published by Alaska Council of Churches, 1967

FOREWORD

I realize I am being presumptuous—for writing an Alaskan history when I am a relative newcomer to the state—for tackling an historical subject when I am not an historian and have not visited any of the original archives—and for writing about Christian missionary efforts when I am not a theologian.

On the other hand, I have tackled this subject with enthusiasm because I have a great love for my new state and its accomplishments, and I want to share with all readers, Alaskan and non-Alaskan, churchgoers and non-churchgoers some of the interesting, courageous, and sometimes amusing stories of the early Alaskan missionaries.

I have had to limit my subject material, much to my great regret, because it has meant the omission (through oversight or lack of time) of many people and events that merit a place in the story. My main emphasis has had to be on the earliest history, when the Church was virtually alone in working to develop the vast Alaskan territory. The countless number of missionaries and church workers who have labored long and hard in the years since 1920, will have to here be on the whole, unnamed.

I only hope that I have whetted the interest of historians and other writers who might now pursue the subject in far greater detail. I also hope that many readers might become sufficiently interested to read some of the fascinating books written by the missionaries themselves. At the end of this booklet I have presented a bibliography which I used for my material, and which gave me many, many hours of exciting reading during this past year.

A word of warning to potential readers and writers of this early historical period—when I first began delving into the books, I eagerly made notes on every available fact. I soon discovered, to my great horror, that there were a number of conflicts between dates and events. Many of these early stories were undoubtedly written down after they had long been passed from person to person, or the source of material may have been an elderly individual with a hazy recollection of dates. In any case, after recovering from my initial shock, I tried to substantiate facts by using two or more sources. When this was not possible, I have attempted to point out to the reader that there is a possible conflict in the material involved.

In conclusion, I want to extend my heartfelt thanks to the Board of the Alaska Council of Churches for their tremendous support, to the members of my advisory committee, (Dr. Meredith Groves, Bert Hall, Herb Hilscher and the Reverend Norman Elliott) for their help in obtaining material and checking facts, and especially to Mrs. Norma Hoyt, also on the committee, for the generous sharing of her large library of early Alaskan books. A special bouquet of thanks to The Reverends A. C. Zabriskie and Hal Banks for their editorial assistance, to Joan Kickbush for creating the cover design, to Joyce Korevec who spent grueling hours coping with my atrocious writing, spelling and grammar while typing the manuscript, and to my husband for his infinite patience while my hand was busy writing instead of keeping house!

ABOUT THE TITLE

In the small village of Allakaket, on the Koyakuk River, eight miles north of the Arctic Circle, there is a little Episcopal Church called St. John's-in-the-Wilderness. A bell was first hung in its steeple in 1907, and Archdeacon Hudson Stuck wrote that the inscription on the bell read "The Voice of One Crying in the Wilderness, Prepare Ye the Way of the Lord."

A family from Anchorage went up to stay in Allakaket during the summer of 1965, and each day, as they listened to the clanging of the bell, they thought of its commanding boom as such a lonely voice, a tiny sound in so vast a wilderness. Curiosity got the better of their fourteen year old son one morning and he climbed to the roof of the church to read the inscription on the bell. "Hey Dad," he yelled, "it reads 'Oh ye Frost and Cold, Bless ye the Lord: Praise Him and Magnify Him Forever'!" What a revelation—no more lonely little voice in the wilderness, but a ringing, booming call to the very elements of nature to magnify their maker.[1]

---

1. The Alaskan Churchman, December 1965, Vol. LX, No. 4. Article by Betty Davey, p. 2.

TABLE OF CONTENTS

Chapter		Page
I	Alaska Under the Russian Flag	9
II	The First American Missions in Southeast Alaska	21
III	Missionaries and Gold Seekers Push to the North	39
IV	First Missions Along the Arctic Coast	61
V	Reindeer and Gold Bring Changes to the Arctic Coast	77
VI	Southcentral Alaska — Children's Homes and Moravians Along the Kuskokwim	89
VII	Alaskan Churches Face New Challenges	103
	Bibliography	123

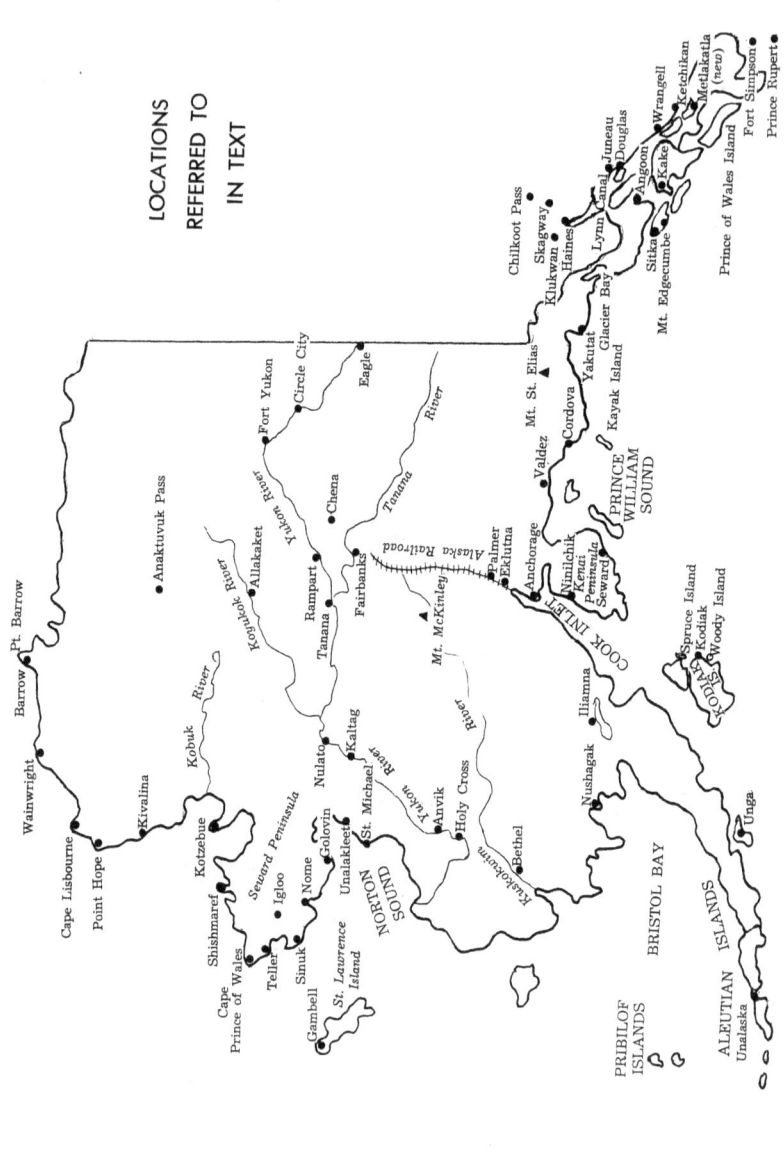

Chapter I

ALASKA UNDER THE RUSSIAN FLAG

American and English traders who sailed about the Pacific Ocean in the Eighteenth Century were aware of a vast northern land in the Western Hemisphere, and referred to it as the "Northwest Coast." Russians had also heard, through Siberian natives of the "Great Land" beyond their bleak shores of Siberia, and it seems strange historical irony that the one European power least concerned with sea travels should be the first to explore the coastline of what is now Alaska, and as late as 1741.

The first Russians to become interested in this northern country were the daring and tough Siberian frontiersmen, descendants of the Cossacks, who had worked their way east from the Caspian region. Their livelihood was the trading of furs and once they had denuded the forests of Eastern Russia, they looked east, toward what might be Siberian America.

Peter the Great was Czar of Russia at that time and was just as anxious to broaden the horizons of his country. In 1725 he called on Vitus Bering, a Danish Captain serving in the Russian navy, to build two ships at Okhotsk in Siberia, and set out to explore the shores across the sea. The Czar was also undoubtedly thinking of being the first to discover the illusive Northwest passage, which so concerned the European traders at that time.

Peter died before the expedition got under way, and it was another sixteen years, in June of 1741, before Bering set sail on a ship named the St. Peter, accompanied by Alexei Chirikof, as Captain of the St. Paul. Alternately buffeted by violent storms and enshrouded by thick fogs, the ships quickly became separated and never found each other again.

Chirikof first sighted land, most historians believe, on about July 15, probably a part of Prince of Wales Island. He landed some of his crew there and they were immediately killed by savage natives. Chirikof sailed on north, following the rugged coastline, but not daring to land again. His log mentions snow-covered mountains and many barren islands extending far to the westward. He returned to the Kamchatka shore in October with twenty-one of his crew dead, and the rest desperately sick with scurvy.

Bering met an even worse fate. He wandered for many weeks until he finally sighted land on July 16th, a towering snow-covered mountain which he named St. Elias. He sent men ashore on what may now be Kayak Island, but they found nothing other than a few deserted sod huts. They sailed on to the westward through terrible weather, occasionally catching a glimpse of the mountainous coast.

Bering and most of the crew became extremely ill from scurvy, and were running out of food and water. It was the final straw when a storm severely damaged their ship, and so they were forced to land on one of the Komandorski Islands, between the Aleutians and the Kamchatka Peninsula. The captain died there, along with many of his men, but a few survived the winter and finally made it back to Siberia the following summer. They had little left in the way of food and clothing, but they did take along the story of their discovery and, most important of all, a small supply of fabulous sea otter and fox furs which greatly excited the frontiersmen of Siberia.

The race was now on for the valuable furs of this new land, called Alaska ("The Great Land") by the Aleut natives who took the full brunt of the stampede of Russian traders. In the next twenty years an average of six ships a summer braved the violent storms of the Bering Sea, wintered among the Aleutian Islands, and returned loaded with valuable furs each spring. The toll of Russian ships and men was frightfully high, but the loss of life among the Aleuts was even worse. The Aleut was a trusting and friendly person, with no warlike tendencies, but when aroused by cruelty and treachery he could repay in kind. The Russian traders treated them as slaves, forcing the men to hunt for the fur-bearing animals and capturing the women to take aboard ship.

The Aleuts told the first Russians that they lived like their brothers, the sea otter—they could journey hundreds of miles over violent seas in their little skin boats, most of their food came from the sea, and their clothing was made from sea animals. Their homes were holes in the ground covered by sod. They had ideally adapted to their environment, but they were no match for the invasion of white men. Historians estimated that fifty thousand Aleuts were living on the Aleutian Islands when the Russians first came. Within fifty years there were only two thousand left.

The slaughter was as hard on the sea otter, the seal and the fox. Within fifteen years these animals had been virtually wiped out in the Aleutians, and the traders had to build larger boats and spend more money in order to travel longer distances along the mainland. Some of the more astute Russian traders, and even government officials in far-away Moscow were becoming alarmed at the ever-increasing reports of bloodshed and the vanishing of the fur animals. They became just as alarmed over another new development—other Europeans had heard about the riches of Alaska and were hastily sending men and ships to explore the area.

The Spanish sent three expeditions north from Mexico, mainly exploring the southeast coastline and Prince William Sound area, leaving Spanish names on all of the charts and claiming land in a number of places. Some of the names remained, present on maps today, (such as Valdez, Cordova, and Port Fidalgo) but not the claims. The Spaniards returned to the south and concentrated on their hold in California.

Captain Cook, sailing for the English, was responsible for many more of the names on the map of Alaska today. In the summer of 1778 he explored much of the coastline, starting in the southeast with Mt. Edgecumbe and sailing north through Prince William Sound to Cook Inlet, then on north past Bristol Bay and Norton Sound to Cape Lisbourne. The arctic ice stopped him there, and he was forced to retreat to Hawaii for the winter, where he was killed by hostile natives. (An English Captain F. W. Beechey, exploring the northern coast in 1826, with his ship bearing the incongruous name H.M.S. Blossom, was also responsible for some of these names.)

Gregory Shelikof, a shrewd Siberian merchant who had played an active role in early fur trading expeditions, was the founder of the first Russian colonies in Alaska. He became the principal stockholder in the company that discovered the Pribilof Islands, the breeding ground of seals, and 1783 he sailed for the Aleutians with three ships, one hundred and ninety two men and his wife—a woman of great energy and business ability, and very brave, too! After wintering in the Aleutians, they sailed to Kodiak Island to set up a permanent colony on the southwest shore, at Three Saints Bay. He could not have chosen a better moment to land there—just at the time of a full eclipse of the sun. The natives thought he was possessed with supernatural powers, and this may have had something to do with the better-than-usual relations between the two groups. Actually the relationship between the Russians and the natives from this time on was not one of continued cruelty—European explorers and traders, including Captain Cook, commented on the way the Russians assimilated with the natives more closely than other early colonizers. To a great degree they lived together with and in the manner of the natives, sharing with one another any small comforts either might be lucky enough to obtain.

The colonists built sturdy homes, planted gardens, and Shelikof himself started a school for the native children. He also claimed that he turned forty heathens into Christians, and appealed to the Russian government to send out missionaries. Catherine was Empress of Russia at that time and showed great interest in the Alaskan developments. In 1788 she granted exclusive control of all Alaskan trading activities to Shelikof's Russian American Company, and also signed an imperial order that missionaries should be sent to the American colonies. Shortly afterwards eleven monks sailed for Kodiak under the leadership of Archimandrite Joasaph, an elder in the order of Augustinian Friars.

The work of the Russian Orthodox Church in Alaska really got under way when Alexander Baranof took over the management of Russian colonies. Sheilkof decided to return to Siberia, to concentrate on consolidating his trading enterprises, and so in 1790 he chose Baranof, a fellow Siberian merchant to take over the running of the colonies. By this time the

The Russian Orthodox Church at Eklutna, a few miles north of Anchorage, is over 104 years old. The graveyard is in the foreground.
(Photo courtesy of Mac's Foto, Anchorage)

The Russian Orthodox Church at St. Michael on the Bering Sea.
(Photo courtesy of Mac's Foto, Anchorage)

The Russian Orthodox Church on the hill above the village of Ninilchik, on the Kenai Peninsula.
(Photo courtesy of Mac's Foto, Anchorage)

St. Michael's Russian Orthodox Cathedral in Sitka burned to the ground in 1966.
(Photo courtesy of Mac's Foto, Anchorage)

Kodiak settlement was thriving and two smaller colonies had been started at Cook Inlet and Yakutat. Baranof was an able and liberal minded leader, with broad experience—in many ways ideally suited for taking on the extremely difficult task of developing the colonies and starting new ones under such adverse circumstances. He spent the next thirty years living in the rigorous climate under the harshest conditions, battling the constant problems of lack of supplies from a far-away homeland, frequently hostile natives, and the ever-present threat of encroachment from other countries.

Baranof was also a controversial personality—he felt a great responsibility toward bringing Christianity to the natives of Alaska, but at the same time he did not want the missionaries to interfere with his personal life, or the lives of the other colonists. So these first priests, led by Father Joasaph, (and others to come) labored under quite a handicap. They worked to bring Christianity to the new land with little or no support from their fellow colonists. They complained of Baranof's heavy drinking and rowdy social life, and were continually at odds with the behavior of the other settlers. They also felt they were given insufficient food and housing, and generally being totally ignored. So no wonder there was a lack of zeal among many of these first priests—they were very unhappy with their lot and patiently awaited a chance to return home.

Ten of these eleven did leave just a few years after their arrival, but they never reached their homeland again—their ship wrecked in a storm and they all drowned. The one man who remained on Kodiak, at Spruce Island, was Father Herman, a saintly person who had totally dedicated his life to the Aleuts about him. He lived alone on the small, wooded island for over forty years, died there and a small cross marks his grave there today. There are many stories about his work, his deeds, and his great love for the native people. It is said that when Father Herman first came to Spruce Island, he lived in a cave until he built a little hut which was to be his home for the next forty years. He wore the same clothing both summer and winter—mainly a simple jumper made of reindeer skin. A small bench covered with reindeer skins served as a bed, and for a pillow he used two bricks. He ate very little, his food consisting of fish he caught, and vegetables he grew in his garden. His thin body, exhausted from labor and fasting, was constantly weighted down with a fifteen pound "chain-fetters" which he wore next to his skin.

At one time a local evil authority suspected the saintly Father of agitating the Aleuts, and an inspection team was sent to his hut. In their zeal to find evidence one man began to tear up the floor with an axe. "My friend," said Father Herman, "I am sorry you took up the axe, this instrument will end your life." One night, a few years later, savage Kenai natives attacked this man while he slept, and chopped off his head.

The Aleuts of Spruce Island were convinced that Father Herman could talk with all the animals. They told of seeing him feed the bears and other wild creatures. Beneath his hut a family of weasels made their home. These little animals are unapproachable when raising their young, but Father Herman fed them out of his hand. The Island inhabitants also say that when he died, all the birds and animals suddenly vanished.

Another favorite story among the Aleuts concerns a tidal wave which approached the island one year. The terrified inhabitants rushed to the Father for help. He calmly carried his statue of the Virgin Mary down to the beach, placed it above the high water mark, and then knelt down to pray. After a short prayer, he told the people to return home unafraid: "the waters will not rise beyond the spot where the holy image stands." And the words of the old man came true.

It is said that five years after Father Herman's death in 1842, Archbishop Veniaminof was on a ship having trouble in a windstorm near Spruce Island. The story goes that the Archbishop cried, "if you, Father Herman, have pleased God, let this wind change." Within fifteen minutes the wind did shift and the ship reached harbor safely. In commemoration of the event the Archbishop himself said a requim mass on the grave of Father Herman.[1]

Despite the problems encountered by the first missionaries among the colonists, they were received most warmly by the natives. The first church was built on Kodiak in 1796, and the

---

1. From an unpublished story on Father Herman written by Orah Dee Clark.

Orthodox priests claimed they had baptized twelve thousand natives by that time. Some of the clergy visited the other Russian colonies and it was also claimed that virtually all the inhabitants of the Aleutians were baptized in a few years time. These wide-spread conversions, however, had little if any depth. The people learned to cross themselves and they loved the pageantry of the church services the priests held during very infrequent visits to the many coastal areas. No attempt was made to translate the scriptures or ritual into the native language in the decades before 1835.

Father Juvenal was one of the better known of these early Christian workers who traveled extensively about the new land. A man of great energy, he did much to spread the Russian Church doctrines. Juvenal spent two years in the Cook Inlet area and became the first Russian Orthodox martyr when he was killed by hostile natives at Illiamna. Priests also visited the new southern coastal settlements, and one accompanied Baranof when he started the first southeastern colony at Sitka in 1802. The little community ended tragically a few years later when an Indian massacre wiped out all the settlers. But **the Russians returned, killed or chased off** the natives and rebuilt the village, this time with an impregnable fortress nearby. They called it Novo Arkangelsk, and within fifteen years the town became the center of the Russian colonies. The first church, later called St. Michael's Cathedral, was built there in 1817, a school was started in 1841, and the first Orthodox Ecclesiastical school, which later became a seminary, was begun in 1845.

Father Ivan Venianimof probably did more to build the Russian Orthodox Church in Alaska than any other man. He has been described as a tall, formidable, athletic person, and when he preached the word of God, "all the people listened without moving, until he stopped. Nobody thought of fishing or hunting while he spoke, and nobody felt hungry or thirsty as long as he was speaking—not even little children."[2] He learned both the Aleut and Tlingit languages, translated portions of the New Testament, and wrote an Aleut-Russian grammar. Under his leadership the almost non-existant Orthodox

---

2. History of Alaska, 1730-1885, Hubert Bancroft, Antiguarian Press, New York, 1959, p. 701.

education program was greatly expanded, and the teaching of reading and writing (in Russian) to native children was undertaken by most of the missionaries.

In 1842 the charter of The Russian American Company was renewed for another twenty years, with a clause in it stating that church establishments throughout the colonies should be supported by the Company. In that same year the Holy Synod formed a new diocese to include the four churches and eight chapels of Alaska and others along the coast of Siberia. Father Veniaminof was made the first Bishop, with his headquarters at St. Michael's Cathedral in Sitka. At this time a Swedish Lutheran missionary, a Mr. Winter, came to Sitka at the invitation of the Russian American Company (who also paid his salary) to serve the one hundred and twenty Scandinavians in their employ. A plot of land was given to the Swedish Lutherans to be held perpetually, and it was not included in the sale of Alaska to the U. S. in 1867.

It was a great blow to Orthodox work in Alaska, but a tremendous honor for Veniaminof when he was recalled to Russia for a promotion in 1858, and he eventually became the Patriarch of Moscow, highest office in the Russian Church. From then on the Alaskan mission work went into a decline, which was certainly not helped any by the transfer of diocese headquarters (after the U. S. purchased Alaska) from Sitka to far away San Francisco. When Russia sold the territory in 1867 there were eleven Orthodox priests and sixteen deacons in the colonies, and although this was the end of the activities of the Russian American Company, the Synod of the Russian Church continued to support its missions and schools until the Revolution of 1917. In 1890 the Church reported it had ten thousand communicants in Alaska, with seventeen mission schools. (A 1903 report on education to Congress listed thirteen Orthodox parishes and thirty schools with seven hundred and forty pupils.) The focus of their efforts centered on Sitka, Kodiak, Belkofoki, Unalaska, Ikogmute, St. Michael, and Nushagak.

Nevertheless, the work had lost the strength and spirit developed by Veniaminof, and the most apt description was given by a Russian commission sent to investigate activities of the missions some years after the departure of this dynamic bishop. "If the object of a missionary be only the baptizing of a few natives yearly to show the country that the number of conversions increases, and in visiting so many times a year such of the villages as are situated in close proximity to trading posts, then the colonial missionaries perform their duty with more or less zeal; but if the missionary's duty is to spread among the pagans the teachings of an evangelist, and to strive by word and examples to soften their hearts, to help them in their need, to administer to their physical and moral diseases, to persuade them gradually to lead a settled and industrious life and above all to labor for the education of the children . . . then not one of our former or present missionaries has fulfilled his duty." [3]

---

3. History of Alaska, Bancroft, p. 704.

Chapter II

THE FIRST AMERICAN MISSIONS IN SOUTHEAST ALASKA

The U.S. bought Alaska from Russia in 1867, but then tried to forget as completely as possible that the purchase ever took place. Two detachments of soldiers were stationed in Sitka and Wrangell for a few years, held responsible for the enforcement of law and order in the whole of the vast territory, but without ordinary police jurisdiction. The one U.S. naval ship patrolling Alaskan waters could do nothing without first sending a formal request by mail to San Francisco.

Ten years after the purchase, the Army forces were pulled out to take care of an uprising in Idaho. The natives of Alaska, whose citizenship had been transferred from Russia to the United States without having any voice in the matter at all, were still without law, police or courts. They were also fighting for their very existence against the exploiters of Alaska's natural wealth. Whaling ships off the Arctic Coast were slaughtering the whales and chasing off the walrus, chief food for the Eskimos; commercial fishermen were already depleting all of the waters of fish, and fur companies were doing their share of the damage on the land. Short-sighted individuals and companies could make a quick fortune much more easily by keeping the native people in a state of ignorance and fear. One of their strongest weapons was liquor—with it they could buy anything from a native, and through drunkenness could keep them in complete subjugation.

The Tlingit and Haida Indian peoples of Southeast Alaska were often called one of the strongest and most intelligent native peoples encountered anywhere in the world by Eighteenth Century European explorers. They could find ample food about them at all seasons of the year, and the climate was mild enough so that they did not have to live in underground huts. They had achieved a high degree of law and order among themselves, (although there was constant warfare between the many tribes and clans within the Tlingits in the north and Haidas to the south) but these old Indian laws had been broken down by the coming of the Caucasians. Probably the only other negative aspect of the Indian (and Eskimo) culture was their shamanism religion. Their lives were guided by the teachings and rulings of the witch doctors. And, although the people admitted to the existence of good spirits, they spent their days placating a host of evil ones. These beliefs led invariably to the practice of slavery, witchcraft, and murder.

During those first ten years of American occupation, many appeals for teachers for schools and Sunday Schools were sent out by Army people at Wrangell. The U.S. Government was totally uninterested, and mission boards were suffering from a post-Civil War lack of funds. The strongest plea for help came from Indians themselves. Philip Clah and five other Canadian Tsimpsean Indians had attended a Methodist mission school at Fort Simpson, just across the border in British Columbia, near present-day Prince Rupert. They went to Wrangell in 1876, started the first school and gathered together each Sunday for worship. A Lieutenant Jocelyn, in command of the Army post, supplied them with hymn books, and by mid-winter between two hundred and four hundred Indians attended each of their three services.

A young Army private, J. S. Brown, very much touched by these efforts of the Indians to educate and Christianize themselves, wrote another letter of appeal for help, this time to the military commander of the Northwest, General O. O. Howard. He turned it over to Dr. A. L. Lindsley, minister of the Presbyterian Church in Portland, Oregon. Dr. Lindsley took the letter with him to the next meeting of the General Assembly of the Presbyterian Church and it was placed in the hands of the man who probably did more than any one person to fulfill the responsibilities of the United States to its thirty thousand citizens acquired by Seward's purchase. Dr. Sheldon Jackson was a strong and dynamic leader, with a wealth of experience in establishing missions. At that time, he was superintendent of all U. S. Presbyterian missions west of the Missouri River. He was a man of high ideals, with no patience for those who wanted to compromise, and he became a highly controversial figure as he set out to bring Christianity, education and medical care to all of the native Alaskans.

In the summer of 1877, Dr. Jackson set up the first Presbyterian mission in Alaska, at Wrangell, leaving it in charge of Amanda McFarland, an equally remarkable person, a veteran of missionary work among the Indians of New Mexico. Her courage and faith must have been tremendous—set ashore alone at a squalid fishing village without law and order, the only white woman there, the white men consisting of the collector of customs, a few traders and transient gold seekers.

Mrs. McFarland immediately joined forces with Philip Clah, and with his help she began teaching the day after her arrival. They started the school in an empty dance hall, but when the miners returned from their diggings in the fall, the two teachers were forced to move to an old log house.

One day Mrs. McFarland rescued two young girls from death at the hands of witch doctors, and protected them in her home. Soon more native girls, who were frequently sold by their mothers to white gold seekers in return for a few blankets, were begging to be taken in, and this was the start of Mrs. McFarland's Girls' Home. The story goes that some of the local miners accosted three of the girls in the street one day. The girls coldly turned their backs and marched toward the Home, singing at the top of their voices, "Yield not to Temptation, for Yielding is Sin." One of the miners was heard to say later, "I'll be blanked if I knew there was that kind of Indian girl."[1]

The Indians of Wrangell made many strides forward that winter of 1877, one of the biggest being the calling, by Christian Indians, of a Constitutional Convention to establish law and order within their village. Amanda McFarland was elected Chairman and together they wrote down some just laws for the community to follow, with a local means for enforcing them. So, by the end of her first year there, Mrs. McFarland's role had become one of teacher, preacher, nurse, doctor, undertaker, administrator and mayor. Her missionary work, however, was seriously hampered by a lack of finances and the need for more workers.

---

[1] Hall Young of Alaska, autobiography, Fleming H. Revell, N.Y., 1927 p. 170

Dr. Jackson spent the winter raising $12,000 for the new mission, from Presbyterian Churches all over the United States, and the next summer he sent the Reverend S. Hall Young, a young missionary from West Virginia, just out of seminary, to help Mrs. McFarland. He also sent the Reverend John Brady and Miss Fannie Kellog to Sitka to start a school there. (Brady later resigned to become a prominent Alaskan businessman, and was appointed Governor of the Territory of Alaska for three terms from 1897 to 1907. Sheldon Jackson returned himself in 1879, and helped build a schoolhouse in Sitka, a new home for Mrs. McFarland's girls at Wrangell, and the first church building at Wrangell. On his return to the States after that visit, Jackson submitted a lengthy report to the Treasury and Interior Departments, requesting that Congress appropriate funds for education in Alaska. $50,000 had been set aside for Alaskan schools in 1870, but it was never used because no means of administering it was provided. Jackson argued that since over a quarter of a million dollars came to the U. S. each year from the lease of sealing rights on the Pribilof Islands, some of this should go toward the schools promised ever since Seward's purchase.

Meanwhile the missions at Wrangell and Sitka continued to grow: by the fall of 1880, Mrs. McFarland was sheltering and training twenty-eight native girls in the Home, and the separate day school included boys, too. The Reverend S. Hall Young was a strengthening and fearless addition to the Wrangell mission. One of his first tasks was to wage a dangerous but successful campaign against witch doctors, breaking their stranglehold on the people. He was also successful in wiping out slavery and became a powerful arbiter between Southeast tribes and clans—their warfare giving way to peace within a few years time. (This fighting between clans and the families which composed them, was frequently over better hunting or fishing grounds, but much of it was also a senseless feuding based on an 'eye for an eye' and a 'tooth for a tooth' system of law. If John killed Jack's brother, then Jack was obligated to seek revenge and before the carnage was over, whole families could be wiped out).

Young traveled frequently all over Southeast Alaska, usually in small Indian canoes, making converts wherever he went. His most successful "conquest" took place just six months after he arrived—he met and married Miss Kellog, the new mission teacher at Sitka! Together they were to devote the rest of their lives to mission work in Alaska.

Some of Young's most extensive trips were shared with the great naturalist John Muir. The two discovered and charted many unknown corners of the Southeast coast, including Glacier Bay. They were the first white men to set eyes on Mt. Fairweather, Mt. Crillon and the other snowy giants of the Glacier Bay area. They were both greatly awed by these peaks and the gigantic, active glaciers beneath them. For the next twenty years, their chart was the only one of this bay, and the largest glacier there still carries the name "Muir."

On their first journey together, the two men covered eight hundred miles in six weeks, all in a small canoe, and aside from geographic explorations, and the study of flora and fauna, they also visited thirteen towns and thirty camps belonging to seven Tlingit tribes. Few of these people had ever heard the Christian message before, and warmly welcomed the men. They were eager for teachers and missionaries, and a number of new Presbyterian missions were begun as a result of this first visit by Young. He recognized the strategic importance of the point of land at the head of the Lynn Canal, recommending a mission (begun in 1881, and named Haines, after the secretary of the Woman's Executive Committee of Home Missions) for that area, and was in Juneau at the time the first prospectors found gold. The Northern Light Presbyterian Church, built there in 1881 and continuing to the present, was the second church built in Alaska for non-natives (the first being the one begun for Russian-Finnish Lutherans in Sitka in the 1840's and abandoned after the purchase). While in Juneau in 1881, Young was also instrumental in calling the first Alaskan Territorial Convention and served as Secretary of the meetings. Besides drawing up local laws, the convention lent their full support to Sheldon Jackson's campaign to sell Congress on the great need for a territorial government.

As Young devoted more of his time to expanding Presbyterian work, the already established missions were continuing to grow. The school at Sitka, started by Miss Kellog and closed down when she married S. Hall Young, was reopened in 1880, including an Industrial Training School, and over the years developed into the Sheldon Jackson Junior College, one of the leading educational institutions of the state today. (In 1884, after a tragic fire, the McFarland Girls' Home of Wrangell was moved to Sitka to join with the boys' boarding school there.)

A number of the young Indian graduates of this institute became Christian leaders in their communities. One of the most outstanding of these students was Frances Phillips, a Tlingit girl from Haines. She fell in love with Sam Johnson, who ran away from his village of Angoon to get an education at Sitka. His people, the Hoochenoos, were the last of the great southeastern tribes to accept Christianity, and the first to learn how to make their own liquor. The rum they concocted from molasses was called Hootchenoo, and later was shortened to "hootch," the word which now means "home brew."

Frances and Sam Johnson decided that the Christianizing of the Hoochenoos would be their life's work. Moving to Angoon in 1885, Frances took virtual charge of the town and its morals. She instructed the mothers in the care of babies, taught the teenagers morality and decency, and she and Sam between them converted the entire village. Frances died soon after her efforts had become successful; Sam, who was studying for the ministry, and fellow Indians, built a beautiful church as a memorial to her.

Two other Indian women, graduates of Mrs. McFarland's Home, and active in the spread of Christianity throughout Southeastern Alaska, were Frances Willard and Mrs. Tillie Paul. Frances, a Tlingit Indian, was sent to school in New Jersey, and returned to teach at Sheldon Jackson's Sitka school. From 1894 to 1897, she was sent to the mission at Haines as teacher and interpreter. She then returned to the Sitka school and spent the rest of her life there, a shining example to the boys and girls of what education and Christianity could bring to their lives.

Tillie Paul was thirteen when Mrs. McFarland opened her Wrangell school and Tillie was among the first to go to the mission building and beg for education. She was a beautiful girl, and at one point, her family stole her from the school to sell her to a white man for a good price in blankets. She escaped and returned to Mrs. McFarland. Four years later, she married Louis Paul, a native Christian of the southern Tongass Indian tribe and they went to live as teachers among the warring people of the Klukwan village. After Louis was drowned on a canoe journey, Tillie spent eighteen years teaching sewing and cooking at the Sitka school. She also helped translate the Bible into the Tlingit tongue. When the Presbyterian Church at Wrangell was without a minister in 1904, Tillie returned there to preach in the language of her people. For the next nineteen years, the mission prospered under her leadership and from there, at sixty years of age, she went on to start a mission at Kake and then take charge of the one at Petersburg. What dynamic women these early Christian Indians!

Sheldon Jackson's many devoted and able helpers would have been seriously hampered in their work without the financial support he supplied during those early years. He traveled constantly all over the United States, making hundreds of speeches, writing endless newspaper and magazine articles, pleading for money and workers to support his missions. He also wrote numerous reports to Cabinet members and Legislators, and appeared in person before committees of the 46th, 47th, and 48th Congresses. Through his influence (Jackson was Alaska's number one lobbyist), the Post Office Department drew up a contract to establish a mail service to Alaska—a big step forward, even though the mail route between Southeast communities was first manned by Indians in canoes!

Dr. Jackson continued to bear down with his one-man campaign to bring an educational system to Alaska and his efforts were rewarded in 1884. Congress finally passed a Civil Administration Law, which was very weak but the best the law-makers would come up with. Alaska was made a "District" (a civil, judicial and land district—previously this term merely included customs and military), with provision for a minimum form of Civil government and a limited education administration. An appropriation for $25,000 (a token in view of the job to be done) was included for public education, and in 1885, the U. S. Commissioner of Education appointed Jackson as General Agent for Education in Alaska.

No school administrator ever faced more difficult problems. Many of the newcomers to Alaska were concerned about church-controlled schools, fearing that Jackson would favor native children over the very small Caucasian minority. He was also faced with the geographic problem of Alaska's great size—individual schools were four and five thousand miles from his headquarters (I am uncertain just which "home base" Jackson was using at this particular time—he traveled constantly throughout his many years of service, at various times calling Sitka, Seattle, and Washington, D. C. his headquarters), and supplies and building materials had to move that same distance. When Jackson became administrator, no public school building existed in Alaska. Therefore, with the small budget at hand, he chose to follow the policy of the U. S. Department of Indian Affairs at that time—to use mission schools wherever possible to save money. A further headache for Jackson was the attempt by the Federal Government, when establishing the District, to apply a school system existing in the States to a region with completely different needs. He tried to offset this by creating three Alaskan school districts. When this failed, because of the great distances between settlements, Jackson tried setting up town school boards. Non-native Alaskans had been complaining about no "home-rule," but this scheme also failed at that time because the people wanted to be paid to serve on the boards, and there were no funds available.

As Jackson was attempting to set up a workable system, he ran into increasing opposition from some of the new District officials. These were politicians from other states, appointed by political motivation rather than for ability or knowledge of Alaska — men mainly interested in keeping outside-vested interests happy and also determined that alcohol continue to flow freely throughout the area. (From several books on this period, I gather that drinking was the main occupation of these officials!). One of the most dramatic and colorful incidents involving the clash between these men and Jackson occurred in Sitka in 1885. Grover Cleveland had just become President and Jackson decided to return to Washington to appeal for the appointment of more able officials. The night before his ship left Sitka, a tourist in the local hotel overheard a plot being hatched by the U. S. Commissioner and the U. S. Marshall to

Amanda McFarland

The Rev. S. Hall Young

The Rev. Sheldon Jackson
(Photos courtesy of the Presbyterian
Board of National Missions)

William A. Kelly, Superintendent of Schools for southern Alaska; Sheldon Jackson and Governor John S. Brady—Washington, D. C., 1905.
(Courtesy of the Presbyterian Board of National Missions)

The Sheldon Jackson school campus, 1882.
(Courtesy of Sheldon Jackson Junior College)

Presbyterian Church and McFarland Home, Wrangell, Alaska, 1881.

The Presbyterian Mission at Haines, Alaska, 1881.
(Reprinted with permission of Presbyterian Board of Publications. Photos from "Life in Alaska," by Frances Williard)

Main Street, Sitka, Alaska, 1881.
(Reprinted with permission of Presbyterian Board of Publications.
Photo from "Life in Alaska," by Frances Williard)

William Duncan, the early 1900's.

William Duncan in 1857.

(Reprinted with permission of
Bishop A. Raymond Grant.
Photos from the "Metlakatla
Christian Mission")

Philip Clah

The Duncan Memorial Church, the "Westminster Abbey of Alaska," was destroyed by fire December 18, 1949.

(Reprinted with permission of Bishop A. Raymond Grant. Photos from the "Metlakatla Christian Mission")

jail Jackson until after the last fall steamer had sailed. They then would have six months of free play until the educator could again communicate with the outside world. The next morning Jackson was arrested at the gangplank of the ship on a trumped-up charge of "obstructing a public highway" (he had laid down a sidewalk in front of his school which crossed an old path used by early Russians, but in disuse since then). The tourist had been unable to forewarn Jackson, but the moment he reached Seattle, he sent word to the Secretary of the Interior. A U. S. Cruiser was immediately sent to Sitka to release Jackson and arrest the two officials.

In tackling the tremendous job of bringing education to Alaskans, Jackson knew that the Presbyterian Board of Missions could not take on any more than they were already committed to (by 1890, they were supporting eight mission schools in Southeast Alaska, with over five hundred students, and by 1912, they had taken on eleven more, including those on the Arctic Coast). Therefore, in 1885 (I am uncertain as to the accuracy of this date) he decided to call a meeting with representatives of other interested denominations to seek their support. At this session, several churches agreed to take on mission work in different areas of the vast territory. Baptists would begin in Kodiak and the Cook Inlet area; Episcopalians would continue work already begun by Canadian Anglicans along the Yukon, and also help along the Arctic Coast; the Methodists planned to begin mission work in the Aleutian Islands, the Moravians would start in the Kuskokwim region; the Congregationalists, the Cape Prince of Wales area, and Presbyterians would continue in Southeast and along the northern Arctic Coast. This agreement to join in the sharing of the work in different areas was a tremendous boost to the development of Alaska, but because it was a broad and unofficial arrangement, it did not preclude the starting of churches in any area where incoming people from the States wanted to have their own denominations.

Before 1898, denominations other than Presbyterian had begun work in the Southeast. Father John Althoff became the first resident Catholic Missionary at Wrangell in 1879. He went on to Juneau the following year, where the first Catholic Church was built in 1885. A hospital and school were set up at the same time by the Sisters of St. Ann. Karl Hendrickson and Adolph Lydell, Swedish Covenant missionaries, went to Yakutat in 1888, setting up a mission with a children's home and school.

The most unusual of these other early missions was the one started by William Duncan at Metlakatla. In response to an English sea captain's plea for help for the warring Tsimpsean Indians along the Canadian Northwest coast, the Church Missionary Society of England advertised for someone to go as a missionary to this hostile people. William Duncan was a young English drygoods clerk, possessing no knowledge of theology, but with a deep religious conviction, and volunteered to return with the captain on his next North Pacific trip. Duncan arrived at Fort Simpson in 1857, and his first contact with the Indians was through Philip Clah, the man who played such a large role in the mission work of Wrangell. Clah taught Duncan the Tsimpsean language and helped him start a school at Fort Simpson.

It took a while for Duncan to gain the friendship of all the Indians—one story tells of a powerful chieftain rushing into the schoolroom brandishing a sword. Duncan was alone, and sure he was about to be killed. The chief came forward, but suddenly stopped, looked terror-stricken, dropped his weapon and ran. Duncan turned around to look behind him and there was Clah, with a six-shooter in his hand. His Indian friend had just been warned of the planned murder, and arrived in the nick of time.

Duncan eventually won many followers, but realized that he would not be able to readily achieve his purpose in coming unless he could establish a "Christian Village" for his converts. So, with the help of the Indians, old Metlakatla, Canada, was set up—a community where no one could take up residence "unless he agreed to live a Christian, civilized life and would conform to and support Christian customs, educational, industrial, and domestic rules of living, as practiced by standard communities." [2] Duncan provided a school, a church, a place to learn trades and job opportunities for all.

---

2. A Short Story of the Metlakatla Christian Mission, William Duncan Memorial Church, The National Press, Calif., 1954, p. 8.

S. Hall Young visited the town on one of his earliest canoe journeys, and was highly impressed with William Duncan and the way in which he planned and led the community. He wrote the following description in his autobiography: "Each family owned a house—they all looked alike and were painted white, eliminating any jealousy or boasting. Each had a smoke house out back for cooking and drying fish, a vegetable garden nearby, and a flower garden out front. There was a building for cabinet making, weaving, and basketry; a large council house, a jail, a school house, and a guest house. The church was in the middle of all and could seat one thousand worshipers. Its bell woke the people in the morning and sent them to bed at night. No white man was allowed to camp within four miles of the village, and a native force rigidly enforced the local laws." [3]

The town grew to include one thousand Indians, and flourished for the next thirty years. Then, high officials of the English Church Missionary Society began to insist on more worship formalities. (A clergyman gave me a more detailed interpretation of this "worship formality" conflict: he said that Duncan was extremely unwilling to baptize anyone, and never children, unless he was sure that the person was fully accepting Christianity. He was even more particular about Confirmation and administering the sacrament of Holy Communion. Duncan felt that talking about Holy Communion as the Body and Blood of Christ could be misinterpreted and have an undesirable effect on a people so recently converted from cannibalistic ways.) Also, government officials began to seriously think about restricting Canadian Indians to reservations. Duncan was very unhappy about this growing "outside" interference. In 1887, through his friendship with Dr. Henry Ward Beecher, eminent U. S. Congregational clergyman, and Episcopal Bishop Phillips Brooks, of Massachusetts, Duncan obtained a hearing with President Cleveland and Congressional leaders. As a result, the Metlakatla Indians were officially granted refuge on any nearby island they chose. The Tsimpseans scouted the adjacent Alaska Territory and picked Annette Island for their future home. There they found plenty

---

3. Hall Young of Alaska, p. 246.

of trees for houses and fuel, lakes for water, a good harbor, and an ample supply of fish for food supply and a profitable industry.

In 1887 over eight hundred people moved from the old Metlakatla to the new, crossing the border from Canada to the United States. They had support from no one mission, but from many friends, and with the help of Duncan's continued inspiring leadership and tremendous faith, modern Metlakatla grew into an even stronger community. The new church was large and beautiful, often called "Alaska's Cathedral"; two schools were built, one for boys and one for girls; salmon canning and boat building kept everyone busy; and the people continued to learn about self-government and life under law and order. They, themselves, earned and spent about $100,000 a year. They kept up their town and made their own improvements, operated their own schools and cared for their sick. Metlakatla could be no greater monument to William Duncan, who died there in 1918, after sixty years of work among the Tsimpsean Indians.

The Metlakatla Christian Mission, made up of village leaders, has continued to carry on his work to this day. Missionaries from the Society of Friends, the Congregationalists, and Methodists have been called on to help over the years, and in 1944, the Mission affiliated with the Methodist Church in an advisory relationship.

Chapter III

MISSIONARIES AND GOLD SEEKERS PUSH TO THE NORTH

The stampede of the gold seekers at the end of the century brought with it the beginnings of a number of churches and missions along the routes to the Alaskan interior and in the many mining towns sprouting up throughout the north. Before the gold rush had begun, however, Anglican, Episcopal, and Catholic priests had braved the great isolation and frigid temperatures of the interior to start missions along the Yukon River.

Church of England missionaries first entered Alaska from Canada following the building of the Hudson's Bay Post at Fort Yukon. In 1862 Archdeacon Robert McDonald, a Scotsman who spent fifty years working among Yukon Indians, went to live at Fort Yukon. While there he translated the Bible, Hymnal and Book of Common Prayer into the Tukudh dialect of the Athabascan Indians. By 1869, Bishop William C. Bompas from the Canadian diocese of Selkirk, and three other priests, all of the English Church Missionary Society, were at work in, or regular visitors to the Fort Yukon area. When the first American Episcopal Bishop, Peter Trimble Rowe, came to Fort Yukon in 1896, he found that Christianity was well entrenched there—the Indians were familiar with the Bible and Prayer Book in their own language. In order to illustrate the depth of faith he found, the Bishop used to tell the story of the Indian he encountered on a distant trail when he first traveled through the region. The Indian had been overtaken by a violent storm and became frightened. "What did you do then?" Bishop Rowe asked him. "I knelt down, prayed to God, and then went on," was the straight-forward reply.[1]

The two earliest Episcopal missions on the Yukon were at Anvik and Tanana. The Anvik work began as a direct result

---

1. The Man of Alaska, Thomas Jenkins, Morehouse-Gorham Co., New York, 1943, p. 112.

of the meeting between denominations called by Sheldon Jackson. The Foreign Missionary Society of the Protestant Episcopal Church agreed to provide a teacher for a school in the lower Yukon Valley. The Reverend Octavius Theodore Parker was sent to St. Michael, at the mouth of the Yukon in July of 1886, and after spending the winter looking for a suitable location, he selected Anvik, an Indian village approximately three hundred and fifty miles up the river. The Reverend John Chapman took his place the next summer, and Anvik became home for the Chapman family for the next sixty-one years, a unique record in Alaskan mission history— John's son, Henry, became a priest, and succeeded his father at the mission! A schoolhouse, home and saw mill were erected first, and a church was built in 1894.

The Tanana mission had been started by an Anglican Reverend Canham (despite a great amount of research, the Reverend's first name remains a mystery) and his wife in 1888, in a strategic area—near the junction of the Yukon and Tanana rivers. In 1891, the American Episcopal church was asked to take over the work and the Reverend Jules Prevost was sent to take charge. Canham stayed with him for an extra year to finishing translating the Book of Common Prayer into the native tongue. Meanwhile, Prevost traveled extensively by dog team and boat throughout the area, among thirty-two Indian villages, and set up a school at Tanana, also under contract with the Bureau of Education.

Unlike most non-native settlements in the interior, the village of Tanana did not depend on an adjacent mining camp, but owed its existence to Fort Gibbon. A military post and telegraph office had been built there by the Army because of the strategic importance of the area. The two settlements sat side by side with only a fence in between, the postal authorities of the little town refusing to be called Fort Gibbon, while the Fort was just as stubborn about taking on the name Fort Tanana. As a result, letters addressed to Fort Gibbon were usually lost, and telegrams sent to Tanana were refused. Hudson Stuck, Episcopal Archdeacon of the Yukon and frequent visitor to the area, wrote that regardless of the animosity between them, the town was necessary to the post for two reasons: whiskey and wood! Most of the buildings of Tanana were saloons, and civilian employees of the Post chopped approximately three thousand cords of wood a year.

The first missionaries built their mission buildings at the Indian village three miles from the town. Hudson Stuck's description of this village's problems was as concise as the reason for the existence of the town: "The evil influence which the town and the army post have exerted upon the Indians finds its ultimate expression in the growth of the graveyard and the dwindling of the village." [2]

The first efforts by the Roman Catholic Church to bring Christianity across the border from Canada were crowned with drama and tragedy. In the summer of 1872, Bishop Clut and Father Lecorre traveled down the Yukon from Canada to St. Michael. Lecorre remained for the winter, but left the next spring when Alaska was assigned to the jurisdiction of Bishop Charles Seghers of Vancouver. Over the next four years Seghers made several journeys to various sections of the Territory, but he was transferred to Oregon before he could enlarge upon his first efforts. He never gave up his dreams of evangelizing in Alaska, and finally went directly to the Pope for reassignment to Vancouver. In July of 1886, he returned to the Yukon, via the Chilkoot trail, taking with him two Jesuit priests and a layman, Francis Fuller. The Jesuits were to spend the winter among the Indians of the Upper Yukon, while the Bishop and Fuller, accompanied by two Indian guides, planned to travel down-river to Nulato. They were caught by violent winter weather and pushed on under great hardship. The strain was too much on Fuller, and the following description, written by a Catholic Sister who had worked with the Bishop, graphically describes the scene that followed:

> "In the wretched hut at Yissetlatch, the humble Archbishop spread the bear's skin which served him for a bed during all his journeyings. The Indians settled themselves on the opposite side, and Fuller was not far from the Archbishop. During the night, Fuller was restless and got up twice. The Archbishop asked him to lie down and try to sleep.

---

2. *Ten Thousand Miles with a Dog Sled*, Hudson Stuck, Charles Scribner's Sons, New York, 1915, p. 152.

"Towards morning, Fuller left the cabin saying he was going to hunt fuel for the fire. He did so and, at the same time, took his gun from the sled and re-entered the hut. He found one of the Indian guides already up and to get rid of him, sent him to fetch some ice to melt and heat for their tea. The other Indian was awake but still wrapped in his blankets.

"Fuller threw a large handful of birch bark on the fire to make a bright blaze, at the same time calling loudly, 'Archbishop, get up!' He added some words that the guide did not understand. The Archbishop raised himself to a sitting position on the rug, and seeing the levelled rifle, took in the situation at once. Crossing his hands upon his breast, he bowed his head in an act of supreme resignation, as the assassin fired. The bullet grazed the heart of the heroic missionary and he died instantly." [3]

Nearby Nulato Indians, who had known the Archbishop, took the body to St. Michael, and escorted Fuller there, too. He was taken on to Sitka to stand trial, but received a relatively light sentence of ten years imprisonment due to his insanity plea. Near Nulato, a white iron cross now marks the site of the tragedy, and a nearby stone outcropping is called Bishop's rock.

Fathers Tosi and Robout, the two Jesuits left behind, did not learn of the tragedy until they reached St. Michael the following spring. They carried on with the Bishop's dream, setting up two missions that year at Nulato and Holy Cross. In the next few years, they were joined by other Catholic missionaries, including Sisters of St. Ann, and a number of missions came into being in this lower Yukon area. (By 1906, Catholic missionaries had begun nine boarding schools, three day schools and four hospitals in the territory.) Education also became an important part of their work, and Holy Cross developed into a model mission, with a large boarding school for both boys and girls. The children were surrounded by a highly self-contained community, including a farm, with cows for plentiful milk, an ample supply of vegetables, a saw mill, small hospital and steamboat.

---

3. The Voice of Alaska, Sister Mary Calasanctius, Sisters of St. Ann Press, Quebec, 1935, p. 42.

Sister Mary Calasanctuis, who wrote about Bishop Seghers, also had many interesting and amusing stories to tell about those early years at Holy Cross. When the Sisters first arrived at this mission, they had to live in a tent. Their Jesuit companions were able to erect two small log dwellings just before winter set in. One morning, a few weeks after the snow had come, the Sisters awoke to find themselves overrun by mice. No amount of setting mouse traps ten times daily could keep up with the rodent propagation, and women finally began wishing for a German pied piper to rid them of the plague. One Sister remembered St. Gertrude, also from Germany, and they immediately began a novena of prayer and penance in her name. Astonishingly, on the ninth day all the mice vanished, as quickly as they had first appeared. The Sisters rejoiced at the miracle, until next morning when Jesuit Father Tosi arrived at their door with the news that the men's cabin had suddenly been overwhelmed by hoards of mice! [4]

Many of the early missionaries were linguists, and some of the Catholic Jesuits became highly proficient in the Indian dialects of their lower Yukon area. Father Robout wrote three grammars for their schools, and others translated prayers and Catholic religious works. Father Jette gained such a mastery of the Indian dialect that, it is said, even the chieftains traveled many miles just to hear him speak in their own language.

The enormity of the language communication problem facing these interior Alaskan missionaries is almost unbelievable. The Indians of this vast northern interior were Athabascan peoples, one large family, but with at least 58 or 59 different language stocks among them, and hundreds of different dialects. In other words, the people of one interior village were frequqently unable to communicate with another settlement just one hundred miles up- or down-river. So, a clergyman's translation of prayers at Fort Yukon was of no value at all to fellow workers at Tanana or Holy Cross. Also, the missionaries were the first people to put the Indian (and Eskimo) dialects into written form, and once that was done, they had to teach the natives to read their own language.

---

4. The Voice of Alaska, Sister Mary Calasanctius, p. 93.

Father Jette wasn't quite as proficient at handling the mission steamboat, however, or so one gathers from reading some of his early letters to his superiors. In 1898, he journeyed from St. Michael to Nulato and from his descriptions, it seems he found and sat on every sand bar in the river. He wrote "the tides in the Bering Sea set at defiance all the most confirmed laws of ancient and modern science . . . there is only one high tide in every twenty-four hours, and this as a rule during the night. So, to wait for high tide meant a stop (on a sand bar) of twelve hours at least."[5] His further descriptions of battling violent wind and rain storms, hoards of hungry mosquitoes, (a much greater hindrance to summer travel than the extreme cold of the winter), vicious currents, and the constant need for cords of wood to keep the boat going, make one fully aware of the difficulties in traveling between missions, even in the summertime. At one point, on this same journey, Father Jette talked of watching a lame Indian walking along the river bank beside the boat, but actually making faster time. He had further woes when he agreed to take on a local Indian as a pilot. After starting up river, and wondering why the boat was so crowded, he discovered that this agreement also included the Indian's wife and children, and his father and mother, too.

The early missionaries found winter travel by dog team more challenging in other ways, but they faced the rigors of the climate and terrain with an eagerness and proficiency that was truly extraordinary. The first Episcopal Bishop, Peter Trimble Rowe, was over forty when he came to Alaska in 1896, but he spent many winter days on the trails with his dog team, usually alone. His most arduous journey was a 350-mile solo trek from Fairbanks to Valdez, in the days before the trail was well traveled by gold seekers. Mushing daily and camping out in minus 60 degree temperatures at night, it took him eighteen days. Eight days out of Fairbanks he ran low on food, and was forced to shoot three of his dogs.

The Bishop had a great sense of humor, which was especially evident when he dipped into his treasure house of trail stories. In all the years he was mushing, he was robbed

---

5. A Letter of Father Jette to Very Rev. Father Rene, Woodstock Letters, p. 179. (Courtesy of the Reverend Paul O'Connor).

Peter Trimble Rowe, D.D., first Episcopal Bishop of Alaska—1895.
(Photo from "The Alaskan Missions of the Episcopal Church," by Hudson Stuck)

First Presbyterian Church in Juneau—before 1890.
(Courtesy of The Right Rev. William J. Gordon)

The first mission house built by the Episcopal Church in Anvik—1887.
(Photo from "The Alaskan Missions of the Episcopal Church," by Hudson Stuck)

The Rev. John W. Chapman, D.D.

The Rev. Jules L. Prevost

(Photos from "The Alaskan Missions
of the Episcopal Church,"
by Hudson Stuck)

At the door of the Episcopal hospital in Circle City—1896.

Stampeders passing through Skagway—1898.
(Photos from "The Alaskan Missions of the Episcopal Church," by Hudson Stuck)

**Hudson Stuck, D.D., Episcopal Archdeacon of the Yukon—
early 1900s.**
(Photo from "The Alaskan Missions of the Episcopal Church," by Hudson Stuck)

The Pelican — the boat used by the early Interior Episcopal Missionaries—early 1900's.
(Photo from "The Alaskan Missions of the Episcopal Church," by Hudson Stuck)

Hudson Stuck conducts a service in the Chapel at Allakaket, using an Eskimo and Indian interpreter—Allakaket probably the only mission serving both an Eskimo village and Indian village.
(Reprinted by permission of Charles Scribner's Sons. Photo from "Ten Thousand Miles with a Dog Sled," Hudson Stuck)

Hudson Stuck has lunch on the trail—at 50 degrees below zero—early 1900's.

Hudson Stuck travels by dog team along the Yukon River—early 1900's.

(Reprinted by permission of Charles Scribner's Sons. Photos from "Ten Thousand Miles with a Dog Sled," Hudson Stuck)

Hudson Stuck conducts a service in an Indian family's home along the Yukon trail—early 1900's.
(Reprinted by permission of Charles Scribner's Sons. Photo from "Ten Thousand Miles with a Dog Sled," Hudson Stuck)

Hudson Stuck and Hary Karstens beginning their descent of Mt. McKinley—1913.
(Reprinted by permission of Charles Scribner's Sons. Photo from "The Ascent of Denali," by Hudson Stuck)

Hudson Stuck Episcopal Hospital—Fort Yukon, early 1900's. Bishop Peter Rowe on the left, with members of the hospital staff.

The Episcopal Church in Tanana—1920 or before.
(Photos courtesy of The Right Rev. William J. Gordon)

St. Matthew's Mission, Fairbanks—early 1900's.

St. John's-in-the-Wilderness, Allakaket. The bell with the legendary inscription.

(Photos from "The Alaskan Missions of the Episcopal Church," by Hudson Stuck

Christ Episcopal Church, Anvik—1894.
(Photo from "The Alaskan Missions of the Episcopal Church," by Hudson Stuck

only once, but when the hold-up man recognized his victim, he insisted on returning the money he had taken. "Why, Bishop, I can't rob you, I'm a member of your Church!"[6] Bishop Rowe also had his share of problems with his dogs. Once, when he was breaking in a new team, the dogs fell through thin ice. After much hard work he finally got them out; later he was asked what he had been saying as he struggled to free them. "God knows, the dogs know, and I know. No one else is ever going to know," was his reply.[7]

Meals on the trail in those days usually consisted of dried fish, dry beans and tea. So it was a great treat for the Bishop and an old sourdough friend when they went to Seattle once and were able to order a steak dinner with all the trimmings. The Bishop was puzzled when the sourdough also ordered a plate of beans. After they were brought to the table, the Alaskan placed the dish on top of his water glass, and said, "There, damn you, watch me enjoy a feast."[8]

When Peter Rowe was first elected Bishop of Alaska by the 1895 General Convention of the Episcopal Church, it was generally understood that his work there would be almost entirely among the native people. But as he made his first journey over the Chilkoot pass, (two years before the great Klondike gold stampede), accompanied by prospectors, gamblers and traders, he realized that his work in Alaska would have to have a double ministry—the new, transient Caucasian population was also in great need of help, especially in terms of hospitals and medical care. The Bishop had tremendous respect and love for these new-comers to the territory. As he traveled with them and lived among them, he continually remarked on the high calibre of the men, their warm-hearted and respectful acceptance of him, their willingness to listen to him, and to come to church services.

They worshiped together out-of-doors, in tents, cabins, and even in saloons when necessary. The Bishop's first service in Circle City, a two year old mining town of over one thousand people, was held in a saloon owned by a Mr. Baldwin, a man of action. He yelled to his customers to down their drinks and

---

6. Peter Trimble Rowe, Mary Cox, Pioneer Builders for Christ Series, The National Council, New York, 1959, p. 13.
7. The Man of Alaska, Thomas Jenkins, p. 186
8. The Man of Alaska, Thomas Jenkins, p. 185

clean the place up. Then, after the sermon, he ordered some of his henchmen to pass the hat, with the command to all to "kick in or else!" [9]

The Bishop elected to return over the long, and difficult Chilkoot Pass route in 1898, in the company of many thousands of prospectors. He chose the hard way (instead of a boat to St. Michael) because it gave him the opportunity to get close to the men, through sharing the work and the hardships of the journey. In return, he gained great respect among the gold seekers—an editorial in an early edition of the Fairbanks News Miner summed up well the feelings of the people for Peter Rowe, "his broad, practical Christianity and sterling manhood have won for him the love and respect of the hard-handed, rough-riding sons of Alaska . . . his works have not been in words but in deeds, and it is the deed, backed by the heart, that carries farthest in a country where the conditions man meets are elemental and always rugged." [10]

The editorial went on to tell of the Bishop's first visit to the new town of Fairbanks in the winter of 1903-04. He saw immediately what was most needed—a hospital. The men of the boom towns and mining camps had no families, and often no friends to care for them when they became ill, and thousands died from diseases caused by filthy, crowded living conditions. The Bishop left some money and said that if the people would build a building with it, he would send in nurses, medicine and furniture the following spring.

So Bishop Rowe placed great emphasis on building hospitals, some with his own hands. The earliest structures were made of logs, with just a few rooms, a small supply of equipment and medicine, usually run by nurses instead of hard-to-get doctors. The Circle City hospital was first, followed by the Bishop Rowe hospital at Skagway, one of the largest boom towns at the start of the gold rush trail. He was also responsible for hospitals at Ketchikan, Wrangell, Valdez, Fairbanks, Iditarod, Tanana and Fort Yukon. Some were short-lived, closing down when the boom towns faded, others carried on for many years, eventually being turned over to the community.

---

9. The Man of Alaska, Thomas Jenkins, p. 185
10. The Man of Alaska, Thomas Jenkins, p. 105

The early Catholic missionaries recognized the great need for medical care, too, and aside from dispensaries at their smaller missions, they also built hospitals in the mushrooming towns. The Catholic hospitals in Fairbanks, Juneau and Ketchikan were later taken over by the Sisters of Providence and are the only facility of that kind in these towns today. The Sisters of Providence opened a one hundred bed hospital in Nome at the height of the gold rush there, to help take care of over two thousand miners and the large native population. One of those eight nursing nuns, Sister Mary Romauld, told the story of what they did when they ran short of funds—the Sisters would slip on fur parkas, harness up their dogs and mush over one hundred miles to lucrative mining camps to ask for money to keep the hospital running. She also wrote of the great hardships of the winters: once she remembered over twenty feet of snow on the ground between the rectory and the hospital. But her summer memories were far more pleasant—gardens and greenhouses loaded with cabbages, carrots, potatoes, turnips, tomatoes and cucumbers, and many of these vegetables could be preserved long into the cold months in a cellar in the sand. The miners and natives kept them well supplied with crab, fish, whale and seal meat from the sea.[11] When the Nome population shrank to below one thousand in 1918, the Sisters closed their facility and moved on to take over the Catholic hospital in Fairbanks.

Both the Catholic and Episcopal missionaries were aware of another great need of the incoming hoards of gold seekers: during the evening hours, the men without families or friends, had little to do with their free time. Many did not want to live at the saloons, and had long since read and reread the small amount of books they had brought with them. Magazines and newspapers were literally worth their weight in gold. So the early missionaries tried to keep an ample supply of reading material on hand, running a virtual lending library in the bush. When the first Episcopal church was built in Fairbanks, the log structure doubled as a reading room. Fifteen hundred books lined shelves in the back, the chancel was curtained off and the pews became benches. At one time over twenty thousand

---

11. North Nun, by Dr. Mike Beirne, Alaska Northern Lights Magazine, September 1966, Volume 1, Number 1.

magazines a year were brought in by boat for the reading room and for distribution in the outlying areas. Later, this library was moved to a separate building, and was maintained by the Episcopal Church until 1941, when it was turned over to the city. A similar reading room facility, called the Red Dragon Club House, was set up in the early days of Cordova, and became a highly popular "hangout." At Tanana, Jules Prevost brought in a small printing press, the gift of Episcopalians in the States, and began publishing the first newspaper in the Alaskan interior, the Yukon Press.

By the beginning of the twentieth century Bishop Rowe was in his sixth of forty-six years of Alaskan work, and had already seen the establishment of thirteen churches, eight schools and three hospitals. Faced with the need to expand Episcopal work all over the territory, especially because of the rapid growth of Fairbanks and other towns, the Bishop brought in a number of new recuits, men and women, for the missions. One of these newcomers was Hudson Stuck, an Englishman by birth, a highly articulate speaker and writer, a forty-year old minister, the dean of St. Matthew's Cathedral in Dallas, Texas. He accepted the post of Archdeacon of the Yukon and the Arctic—living first in Fairbanks and later in Fort Yukon, helping the Bishop by providing closer, more frequent contact with the many communities of the interior.

Hudson Stuck began a series of winter journeys by dog team which covered from fifteen hundred to two thousand miles a year—actually serving or supervising Allakaket, Anvik, Chena, Circle City, Eagle, Fairbanks, Fort Yukon, Nenana, Rampart, and Tanana as well as almost twenty-four smaller missions along the routes. Some of these places which were thriving in the first years of the new century were to disappear by 1920 (Circle City dropped from a population of three thousand to thirty within a couple of years). Stuck, in his usual succinct manner, described the town of Fairbanks in 1904 as "Ten thousand people in the area but no one here to stay." [12]

While Bishop Rowe developed a special kinship with the Alaskan newcomers, Hudson Stuck grew to know and love the

---
12. Hudson Stuck of Alaska, Arthur Ben Chitty, Pioneer Builders For Christ. The National Council, New York, 1962, p. 13.

Indians in a way almost unmatched by any other missionary. He knew well the problems they faced, he insisted on preserving native customs, skills, clothing and food. He condemned as vicious practice the "Americanizing" of natives for profit. He saw the sale of bright cotton clothing bring money to traders, but pneumonia to the Indians, and he saw starvation wipe out whole families because the men hunted for furs to sell instead of meat to eat and then spent all of their money on liquor. The welfare of the natives was always dear to him— he wanted Alaska saved for native Alaskans, and because of this forthright stand, he, like Sheldon Jackson, became a controversial figure to incoming Caucasians.

It is already obvious that Hudson Stuck was a highly versatile man, but he was also a talented author, writing five books on Alaska which are now collector's items, at least fifty magazine articles, and to "top" everything off, he made the first successful climb of the highest South Peak of Mt. McKinley! His companions on this historic ascent in 1913 were Harry Karstens, a prospector, Walter Harper, Stuck's half Indian guide and interpretor, (his father had made the first exploration of the Tanana River in 1878) and Robert Tatum, a twenty-two year old seminarian who later became a clergyman. True to his deep convictions, Stuck called his book about the climb, "The Ascent of Denali," (Denali meaning the "Great One"), and in his foreword wrote "It is now little more than seventeen years ago that a prospector penetrated from the south into the neighborhood of this mountain, guessed its height with remarkable accuracy at twenty thousand feet, and ignorant of any name that it already bore, placed upon it the name of the Republican candidate for President of the United States at the approaching elections—William McKinley. No voice was raised in protest, for the Alaskan Indian is inarticulate and such white men as knew the old name were absorbed in the search for gold." [13] And, so Hudson Stuck, the mountain-climbing missionary, staunch defender of the Indian, made an eloquent plea to restore the native name to Mt. McKinley— Denali.

---

13. "Ascent of Denali," Hudson Stuck; Charles Scribner's Sons, New York 1914, Preface.

Chapter IV

FIRST MISSIONS ALONG THE ARCTIC COAST

Whaling ships from the United States first began to hunt whales in the Bering Sea off the Alaskan coast in 1848. The numbers of ships increased rapidly with each year, mainly hunting the bowhead whale for its baleen—long flexible strips in the whale's mouth which were in high demand for corset stays—a top priority item at that time. Whale oil was also collected for soap and other products. The impact of these whalers on the Eskimo inhabitants of the coast was the usual sordid story—the trading of liquor for whale bone and the bringing of diseases which brought widespread sickness and death.

However, the white man's diseases which brought terror and death to Eskimos only compounded already existant problems: the witch doctors of the north were as wicked and powerful as the shamans of the Southeast Indian tribes. The dean of all medicine men was Attungowruk, a chief of Point Hope. For many years he reigned supreme by declaring whatever laws and taboos he decided were needed. The most gruesome example of his ruthlessness was his highly successful technique for telling newcomers just who was boss. He simply gave them an escorted tour of the village graveyard, where bodies were kept above the frozen ground (in preparation for a mass burial in the summer when the earth thawed), carefully pointing out all the men he personally had done away with.

It is also said that Attungowruk was indirectly responsible for the secret of whiskey-making coming to Point Hope. A white visitor to this area had been badly treated by the witch doctor, and he took revenge by showing local Eskimos how to distill alcohol. Now liquor was readily available all year long, and it was very nearly the undoing of both Attungowruk and his people—when Eskimos drank, they were unable to hunt, and whole families frequently starved to death.

Attungowruk's grab for power, and other men's wives brought about his eventual downfall—he was shot to death in the winter of 1889 in his home, among his many wives.

The U. S. Revenue Cutter Thetis patrolled the waters of the Bering Sea, trying to maintain a semblance of law and order. Its Captain, Commander Charles Stockton, was shocked by the conditions he was continually finding, and appealed to both Sheldon Jackson and the Board of Missions of the Episcopal Church. Jackson had just become General Agent for Education and was making plans to extend schools to other parts of the territory. After the historic meeting with secretaries of other denominations, the Congregationalists and Episcopalians agreed to take on Arctic Coast schools, while the Presbyterians planned to start one up at Barrow.

In the summer of 1890 Jackson sailed north on the Revenue Cutter Bear with the men who were to be in charge of the three missions. Mr. Harrison R. Thornton and Mr. W. T. Lopp, missionaries of the Congregational Church, went to Cape Prince of Wales, a major meeting place for many of the northern Eskimo villages. They were successful in starting a school and mission there, but later, Thornton became one of the few missionaries to be murdered by native Alaskans—shot to death by two drunken Eskimos. Mr. Lopp worked for many years along the Arctic Coast, later becoming superintendent for the U. S. Government of reindeer stations and schools in Northwestern Alaska.

Dr. John Driggs, a medical man and Episcopal layman stepped ashore at Point Hope, a long, flat point of land reaching far out into the stormy Bering Sea, covered only by moss and sand, and during the short summer by a carpet of beautiful miniature wildflowers. There is nothing to break the sweep of the wild winds coming from the Pole. The gales can bring frigid temperatures in the summer, but add much to make living miserable and hazardous during the long winter months when there are many weeks of no sun, and the thermometer reads twenty and thirty degrees below zero.

This Arctic weather gave Dr. Driggs an extra special greeting on his arrival — while his belongings were being landed, the waves swept away most of his precious coal supply and nearly all of his clothing. Once settled in a two room house which would serve as school and living quarters, the doctor's next problem was to persuade the children to come to classes. This was easier said than done because no one in the village really knew just what a school was all about. The story goes that John Driggs lured his first pupil with a molasses cake, and almost immediately found himself faced with fifty students, all eager to learn to read and write.

These early teachers among the Eskimos faced other problems unique to their area. The people did not know the difference between the days of the week, so they had to be taught how to determine the weekend, when school would be closed. (Dr. Driggs postponed Sunday worship services and classes for several years—until he had truly won the confidence of the people and could communicate with them in their language. But from the moment he arrived at Point Hope, he showed the people the perfect example of a Christian life, through his love for them, and ceaseless work for the youngsters, the sick and those in need.)

A further complication for the teacher, in starting classes, was the problem of time. The Eskimos had no clocks and the school had no bell. And in the Arctic one just can't tell time by the sun, when sunrise varies from midnight to noon in six months time. Also, the number of pupils varied greatly according to the season—when the whales were being hunted, the school was packed with newcomers to the village. When it was time to shoot caribou, there was a mass exodus for the interior and the school was virtually deserted. The school was also emptier on the rare good days, when everyone took off to hunt or fish, and crowded during the stormy weather.

Despite all this confusion, John Driggs' school was a great success, and he was also kept busy with the treating of the sick. For those too ill to come to him, he would make his calls after school hours, often traveling many miles to outlying hunting camps. When he had finished caring for the Eskimos' needs, he still had to hunt for driftwood for fuel, cut ice for his water supply and do a bare amount of cooking and housework.

Dr. Driggs faced many hardships with the people of Point Hope during his eighteen years there. When storms battered the land, waves frequently drove the people from their homes, often in frigid weather. In some years, when winter came early, the annual supply ship could not get through at all. Fuel for heat was a serious problem, and so was an adequate food supply. At one time the only food left in the village was a dead walrus washed ashore during a storm.[1] Tragedy was a part of every day life in the Arctic. During the doctor's first year there, he lost three students to drowning and bears. Another was killed by dogs, and over the years many succumbed to white man's diseases. One year a measles epidemic killed every baby in the village.

A further hardship for the doctor was the total lack of companionship with anyone from outside Alaska. After he had spent four unbroken years there, the Episcopal Church sent up an assistant, the Reverend E. H. Edson. Though Edson stayed only a short while, Driggs turned over the school teaching to him, and the doctor began to make long journeys along the coast, teaching and taking care of the sick wherever he went. One of his frequent stops, just south of Point Hope, was the village of Kivalina, the home today of the first Eskimo Episcopal priest. (Milton Swan was ordained to the Priesthood in 1964).

Word had spread up and down the coast about the many changes taking place at Point Hope: the liquor problem had diminished, the stills had disappeared, polygamy had gone and women were being treated with much greater respect, the old witch doctors' taboos were being abandoned, the school had broadened the intellectual scope of the young people; and some of their parents had learned to read and write enough to protect themselves against unscrupulous whalers and traders. But Dr. Driggs had been wise in the selection of these changes—his goal was to help the people of Point Hope become educated Christian Eskimos, not imitations of the incoming Caucasian Christians. So while the hardships were always there, "the steady growth of the Point Hope people

---

1. John Driggs Among the Eskimos, Mary Cox; Builders for Christ series, The National Council, New York, 1956, p. 10.

in the understanding and practice of the Christian faith was Dr. Driggs' great support against the beatings of discomfort and misfortune." [2]

By 1908, although the Doctor was only fifty-four, his health had failed, and he was obliged to turn over his mission work to others. He found it impossible, however, to adjust to living in the southern states again, so he returned to the Arctic Coast, making his home at Cape Lisbourne, fifty miles north of Point Hope. He spent the last five years of his life there, trapping and hunting for his food and supplies. When he became ill in 1914, his Eskimo friends tried to take him by dog team to the mission at Point Hope. He died while enroute, and was buried near the storm-swept cliffs of Cape Lisbourne.

The same ship that left Dr. Driggs at Point Hope took Sheldon Jackson and Professor Leander Stevenson on to Barrow. The forty-five year-old teacher stepped ashore at Arctic surroundings similar to Point Hope—a flat, sandy point of land wide open to the vicious polar winds, and cut off from the outside world nearly eleven months of the year.

The Revenue Cutter also brought provisions for the Rescue Station, maintained at Barrow by the government to help whaling ships in distress (in the ten years before Stevenson's arrival, about two thousand sailors had been shipwrecked along the Arctic Coast). The mission teacher was given a rear room at the Station for his school and living quarters, and he later took complete charge of this government work. Over the years ahead, the missionaries of this farthest-north post faced the additional burden of feeding and caring for hundreds of shipwrecked sailors.

Professor Stevenson's primary task was to start the school, and he was faced with the same problems which confronted Dr. Driggs. By the end of the summer, he had collected thirty-five pupils and throughout the long, dark winter, he gained the confidence and friendship of all the people. The professor rapidly outgrew his single room, so when the Presbyterian Mission Board sent him some lumber four years

---

2. John Driggs Among the Eskimos, Mary Cox; Builders for Christ series, The National Council, New York, 1956, p. 13.

later, he turned carpenter and built a school house and mission home. When seven years had gone by, and his work was well established, he returned home to his wife and children. Stevenson originally promised the mission board (and his wife) that he would go for one year only!

In 1897 Dr. and Mrs. Horatio Marsh replaced Professor Stevenson at Barrow, the doctor having just married and graduated from a New York medical school. They were welcomed in a most dramatic way—no sooner had they settled into the mission when word came that a whaler had been crushed in the ice just off shore. The doctor went to rescue the captain and crew, and brought them to Barrow. This particular crew was lucky—once fed and outfitted from the Marsh's meager supplies, they were able to take the Revenue Cutter south before winter set in. A few years later, the situation was a lot more crucial. The polar ice came early that fall and crushed eight large ships. More than three hundred seamen escaped with their lives and descended upon the mission. Dr. Marsh filled the station and school house with bunks, built some native-type structures, and eventually he and Mrs. Marsh even had to turn their own home over to the unexpected guests. They moved in with an Eskimo family, and in the midst of all this crisis and chaos, Mrs. Marsh gave birth to a baby, the first white child born on the Arctic Coast.

Dr. Marsh had his hands full treating the sick that winter, but their biggest worry was the shortage of food and fuel. By February, the entire village was facing starvation—there was little left to eat and the shoreline was stripped bare of all driftwood. Marsh had sent out a frantic plea for help with the last whaler to escape the ice, and one day in March, when the community was about to give up all hope, a rescue party arrived on foot, bringing food and medicine. Dr. Jackson had offered to help with a herd of four hundred reindeer which he had raised from Siberian stock, and Lt. David Jarvis, of the Coast Guard Cutter "Bear" and Mr. Lopp of Cape Prince of Wales, volunteered to drive them seven hundred miles north from Teller to Barrow. The reindeer meat, plus caribou that the men had killed enroute, were enough to keep the village going until the next summer's whaling fleet picked up the stranded men.

Dr. Marsh took over supervision of what was left of the reindeer herd, training local Eskimos to care for them, and within a few years, the numbers increased to over five hundred. Never again were the people of Barrow faced with such wholesale starvation.

Obviously, the doctor's activities were greatly varied, like most of the early missionaries—he and his wife kept the school going, he turned to carpentry and built a small church, and when Dr. Jackson secured the first government post office for Barrow in 1901, Dr. Marsh was appointed Postmaster. His main interest, however, was in the medical field, and he worked tirelessly to care for the sick, not only in Barrow, but in many of the outlying camps and villages. He strongly believed that a hospital was urgently needed in that area, and sent annual pleas to the Presbyterian Board of Missions. Unfortunately, he was unable to enjoy the fruits of these efforts. After fifteen years of service, ill health forced the Marshes to leave Alaska— the long dark winters had seriously affected Mrs. Marsh's eyes.

A Presbyterian hospital was built in Barrow in 1920 and Dr. and Mrs. Henry Greist took charge of it until the U.S. Public Health Service took it over in 1936. The Greists were equally versatile in their performance of services for the community. For years, the doctor was the only medical man within a thousand miles and the only preacher within three hundred and fifty miles. Mrs. Greist was a nurse—she had been in charge of a thirty-bed hospital in Montana before coming to Alaska, so she became an indispensible part of the new Barrow facility. She also taught school, organized local mother's clubs, performed the duties of the U.S. Weather bureau, and in her spare time, collected birds' nests and eggs for U.S. museums!

The first Eskimo to be ordained as a minister in the Presbyterian Church, in 1941, was a resident of Barrow—Percy Ipalook (the second was the Reverend Roy Ahmaogak, of Wainwright, ordained in 1947). He received his earliest religious training under the Marshes, spent five years at the Sheldon Jackson School at Sitka, and then four more years in the States for more academic and theological training. He returned to the Arctic Coast to serve his people at Wales and Wainwright as a layworker from 1935 to 1940, and was ordained in Barrow in 1941.

From 1943 to 1945 the Reverend Mr. Ipalook had charge of a mission which could take the prize, not only for the most barren and inhospitable surroundings, but also for the tragedy in its past—St. Lawrence Island, a wind-swept pile of rock in the midst of the stormy Bering Sea, just forty miles southeast of Siberia. In the summer of 1878, traders visited the eight hundred Eskimos on the island and took all the seal and walrus skins in return for liquor. Most of the people were drunk all summer, ignoring hunting and fishing, so when winter descended, they had no furs or food to keep them alive. When the Revenue Cutter paid its yearly visit to the island the following spring, the crewmen could see bundles of fur lying the beaches. When they looked more closely, they realized that the objects were not dead animals but the bodies of people. They discovered with horror that whole villages had frozen to death—approximately four hundred people, or over half the population of the island had died because of the white man's gift of liquor.

Sheldon Jackson heard this story from the captain of the Cutter and resolved to establish a mission on the island to help the survivors of the tragedy. In 1891, he built a school house and a teacher's home there, but it took him another three years to find someone to take over the bleak post. In 1894, the Reverend and Mrs. Vern Gambell were set ashore, and immediately opened the school, which was farther west than any other on land belonging to the United States. Mrs. Gambell arrived as a bride, twenty years old, and the first white woman the Eskimos had ever seen. Her husband had been a teacher and school principal in Iowa for thirteen years, so he had relatively little trouble in successfully handling the problems of the new school. He had more difficulty, however, in overcoming the power of the local witch doctors. One shaman was particularly antagonistic, and when both Gambells developed bad colds, he walked up and down in front of their house casting a spell of death on the two inside. Fortunately for the Gambells they were able to avoid pneumonia, and after a week of anxious doctoring they emerged completely well.

The Revenue Cutter "Bear" in Bering Sea ice near King Island—1892.

(Courtesy of the Presbyterian Board of National Missions)

The igloos at Point Hope—1917.
(Reprinted by permission of Charles Scribner's Sons.
Photo from "A Winter Circuit of Our Arctic Coast," Hudson Stuck)

The Point Hope graveyard—surrounded by a fence of 812 whalebones.
(Courtesy of the Right Rev. William J. Gordon)

Robert Sams, pioneer Quaker missionary. The picture was taken shortly before his death in 1958.
(Courtesy of the California Society of Friends)

The Presbyterian Church and Congregation at Point Barrow. Photographed by Hudson Stuck in 1917.

The actual Point Barrow — the northern extreme of Alaska. Hudson Stuck was the cameraman, in 1917.

(Reprinted by permission of Charles Scribner's Sons. Photos from "A Winter Circuit of Our Arctic Coast," Hudson Stuck)

Natives of St. Lawrence Island, interested in photography—before 1900.
(Courtesy of the Presbyterian Board of National Missions)

The final downfall of this particular shaman was an ignominious one—Gambell noticed that his winter food supply was disappearing at an unusually alarming rate—he set a snare inside the store room and caught the medicine man with his parka full of canned goods. The villagers planned to kill the thief because he had committed one of the worst of all crimes in the northland—stealing from another man's food cache. Gambell saved him from death but the shaman lost face, and his powerful hold on the people.

In the next three years, life improved greatly for the people of St. Lawrence Island, and education caught hold in a big way. Mrs. Gambell gave birth to a baby girl, but in the fall of 1897, she fell and injured her back. They were forced to return to the States so that she could have hospital treatment. They took a schooner from Seattle the following spring, most anxious to return to their island home, but the ship sank in a severe storm off Vancouver Island, and all aboard were drowned. The Eskimos of St. Lawrence Island had been watching for weeks for their friends to return, and were greatly saddened by news of the disaster. It is a fitting memorial to a brave couple that one of the two villages on the island now is called Gambell, and that the Presbyterian mission begun by them continues to this day.

Immediately after the tragedy, Vern Gambell's brother, a doctor at a government hospital at Unalakleet, went right to St. Lawrence to take over for his brother. Dr. and Mrs. Edgar Campbell took over the work in 1901 and during their ten years there, greatly strengthened the mission — adding a medical clinic, an orphanage and a church building.

Dr. Jackson was responsible for another early mission along the Arctic Coast. In 1895, the California Friends (Quakers) Church sent missionary Anna Hunnicutt as a teacher to Kake and Douglas in Southeast Alaska. When the young woman first met Dr. Jackson, she told him of her great desire to find an area where California Friends could carry on missionary work. Later that summer, while on his trip along the Arctic Coast, Jackson met with Kotzebue Sound Eskimos. They asked him for missionary teachers to live among them, so the doctor told the group about Anna Hunnicutt.

The Eskimos decided to send a delegation to Douglas right away, and two of the strongest men paddled an open canoe two hundred and fifty miles south to Cape Prince of Wales, where they found a boat going to the Southeast. These two determined young men brought Anna Hunnicutt, and Robert and Carrie Samms back with them the following summer, and the three were given the warmest of welcomes. They found themselves in the midst of the great summer "Rendezvous"— Kotzebue being the trading center, and summer hunting and fishing grounds for the Eskimos of the Kobuk, Noatak, Selawik and Imnachuk Rivers. Traders also came from Nome, St. Lawrence Island, Diomedes and even Siberia.

When the summer visitors were headed for home, the remaining permanent residents of Kotzebue built the three missionaries an 8x10 foot cabin for the winter. Its floor was three feet below the ground, the walls were of lumber brought from the States, first covered with moss and dirt, and later with ice and snow, and a storm entrance was the finishing touch to make it as cold-proof as possible. All during their first winter, the Friends held services in this little cabin, and also went daily into Eskimo homes to give school and Bible lessons.

One day, in the middle of the following summer, the whole village was astonished to find, on awakening, a fleet of thirty-four ships anchored offshore. Some fifteen hundred men and a few women swarmed ashore, all asking one question—where is the gold? Up until then, no one had ever heard of gold in that area. The newcomers were undaunted and planned to settle down for the winter anyway. Among them was another group of Quakers from California who built a cabin and started mission work about one hundred and seventy miles up the Kobuk River. During the following winter, Robert and Carrie Samms (who, together devoted fifty years to Alaskan missionary work) frequently traveled far up the river by dog team, stopping over with the newcomers to break the journey. Once, when they lost their lead dog to poisoning, the young missionary wife traveled forty miles in sixteen hours on snowshoes! [3]

---

3. An unpublished account of the Work of California Friends Church in Western Alaska, by Matilda Hawarth, p. 4.

In 1901, the U.S. Government officially accepted the Kotzebue Friends School, and provided fuel, school room supplies and some compensation to the teacher. In 1904, the Friends field superintendent was appointed U.S. Commissioner and Postmaster, and 1909, the government shipped up building material for a hospital at Kotzebue. It offered to pay a physician's salary, if one could be found, and the Eskimos themselves raised three hundred dollars for this purpose. Dr. Benjamin Newsome, a Friend from California, responded to the call. Later, the Friends also established a Kotzebue high school, the first of its kind north of the Arctic Circle. (When the U.S. Government later took it over, the Friends united with the Evangelical Covenant Mission at Unalakleet to maintain a Christian High School there.)

Chapter V

REINDEER AND GOLD BRING CHANGES TO THE ARCTIC COAST

The importation of reindeer to Alaska plays a controversial role in the State's history. In weighing all the pro's and con's however, there seems to be general agreement that the move did much to save the Eskimos from extinction during those early years after the purchase. Alaska's Senator Ernest Gruening stated, "The most important single contribution made to the (Eskimo) natives . . . in the first half-century of United States rule was the importation of reindeer, which, during the period when the natural food supply had been greatly impaired, saved thousands of Eskimos from death by starvation."[1]

When Sheldon Jackson first journeyed along the Arctic Coast in 1890, he learned about the starvation the Eskimos were facing, thanks to the fact that commercial ivory hunters had slaughtered the walrus, whalers were driving the whales beyond the reach of the native skinboat, and seals were being killed for their skins at a rate that could wipe them out in a few years time. And the U.S. Government was doing nothing to control these large scale operations which were spelling doom for the Eskimos.

During that same trip to the Arctic in 1890, Jackson also visited Siberian coastal villages just across the way. Several years before, a number of American whaling ships had been crushed in the ice off the Cape Navarin coast of Siberia. Native Koriaks had rescued one American, and nursed him back to health. The U.S. Congress voted to reward the people, and Captain Healy, with his Revenue Cutter Bear was given the job of taking one thousand dollars in gifts (cotton material, sugar, tea, tobacco and toys) to the Koriaks.

While on this visit, Jackson was able to observe these villagers and their reindeer economy. He came to the conclusion that this was the answer for the Alaskan Eskimo—he

---

1. The State of Alaska, Ernest Gruening; Random House, N. Y., 1954, p. 359.

felt that not only could reindeer save Eskimo lives, but it could also save their self-respect, bridging the gap from past to future, from huntsmen to herders.

Jackson went right to Washington with his report, asking for a Congressional appropriation, but his plea fell on deaf ears. He then turned to the public, through letters to all major newspapers, and raised over two thousand dollars. It was enough to allow him to return to Siberia the following summer and purchase sixteen animals. The first reindeer were taken to Unalaska, but the experiment was not a success, probably due to the much warmer, rainer climate. Dr. Jackson appealed to Congress once more in 1892, with the same results, and that summer, with private funds again, he made five trips across the Bering Sea to bring back one hundred and seventy-five animals. A reindeer station was begun on the Seward Peninsula, at Teller, named after Senator Henry M. Teller, of Colorado, who had championed Jackson's cause from the beginning.

The Teller experiment was a complete success, and in 1893, and again in 1894, Congress appropriated six thousand dollars. That summer Jackson brought over one hundred and twenty seven more reindeer, while the first Teller herd began reproducing rapidly. Animals were distributed to a number of the northern missions and the project began to show signs of fulfilling Jackson's hopes. A dramatic example of this success—the great climax of Jackson's proof came during the winter of 1898 when a reindeer herd was sent north to rescue the starving people of Barrow.

Congress became more receptive to the plan and, between 1894 and 1908, appropriated over $240,500 for the importation and care of the animals. By 1917, the original herds had increased to about ninety-five thousand (by 1930 they were estimated at six hundred thousand) and besides supplying food (indispensable at times when hunting or fishing were poor) and by-products, the Eskimos had also received an estimated cash income of around $90,000. One further advantage—in 1899 Jackson secured the first Reindeer Post Route in the United States. It ran from St. Michael, on the southern Bering Sea up to Kotzebue, and later went all the way up to Barrow.

The Methodist Church in Nome in 1906.
(Courtesy of the Rev. Howard L. Devore)

The Rev. Sheldon Jackson landing the first reindeer herd at Port Clarence, July 4, 1892.
(Courtesy of the Presbyterian Board of National Missions)

In more recent years all of the herds have declined, and the people of the north did not adopt the reindeer economy as Dr. Jackson had hoped. There are a number of reasons— among them that the reindeer, if not carefully watched, were killed by wolves, or wandered off to join wild caribou herds. But most important, probably is the fact that the coastal Eskimos are relatively sedentary people, their living based on hunting and fishing rather than the nomadic herding of the Siberians or Laplanders. In the spring, for instance, even the best of the herders had to return to their villages for whale hunting and many of their animals would then wander off.

One of the criticisms leveled at the reindeer project was the accusation that the reindeer herds were kept in the hands of the missionaries rather than the Eskimos. But it was obvious to Jackson at the beginning that the animals could not be turned right over to the Alaskan natives without first training those interested in herding. At most of the mission stations, Eskimos worked as apprentices for three years, then were given twenty-five or fifty reindeer of their own. The Sinuk Methodist Mission supervised over 341 reindeer in 1911, half of them belonging to Eskimos, apprentices and "graduates" of the training program.

When Jackson first transported the reindeer to Teller, he also brought along a number of Siberian herdsmen. The arrangement with these Siberians just did not work out—they were unhappy, moody, and irresponsible. They were quickly sent home and Jackson went all the way to Norway to bring back sixteen Lapp herders to train the Eskimos. The leader of the Lapps was William Kjellman, who brought along his father, wife and child. The Lapps agreed to come only on the condition that they be accompanied by a Lutheran clergyman who could attend to their spiritual needs, and also teach their children.

So, at the request of the U. S. Government, the Norwegian Lutheran Synod, asked the Reverend Tollef Brevig, who had served as a school teacher in Minnesota prior to his ordination, to accompany the Lapp families. They all arrived at Teller Station in August of 1894. Brevig and his wife were kept busy from the very beginning with teaching and ministering to both the Lapps and the natives of the area. The missionary, during his eighteen years of service there, became especially close to the Eskimos—he developed a great love for them and a deep knowledge and understanding of their customs and beliefs. The love was obviously mutual—the Eskimos adopted him, not only by warmly accepting his presence, but also in a tribal initiation ceremony. He was given the Eskimo name Apaurak, meaning "The Father of All," signifying the absolute confidence and esteem they accorded him.

Brevig learned that the true native name for the Eskimo people was Innuit, meaning simply "people." The term "Eskimo'" was considered one of reproach, given them by their neighbors. Its meaning is "raw fish eaters." He also discovered that they were an extraordinarily good-natured, deeply religious people, but, like the Southeast Indians, their primitive animism subjected them to demon worship, to the placating of the evil spirits and to constant fear of superstitions. The sick were left unattended, for fear the bad spirit responsible would take over the person helping. For the same reason, the dead were abandoned to wild animals far outside the village and no one could ever be given the name of someone who died.

When Brevig first arrived at Teller, the Eskimos there lived in tents of walrus hide during the summers. This was their time to travel up and down the coast in search of food. During the long winters they stayed put--digging holes deep in the ground for houses, making walls and roofs of drift timber, covered by sod. Each home, (called "igloo" by the Eskimo, meaning "house"), had only one small room, used by from one to four families, or from four to sixteen people. Each family unit was given a private corner, while the cook fire burned in the middle, beneath a small opening in the roof, the only one in the dwelling—the entrance being through a long underground tunnel. Understandably, the smoke and stagnant air were appalling—one of the prime reasons for the high incidence of tuberculosis and other respiratory diseases. At night even the roof hole was closed, and the families slept naked among furs in a totally sealed-off house.

At the turn of the century, the Eskimos of Teller (and all along the northern Alaskan coast) were hit by a terrible measles epidemic. The disease had been brought ashore at Nome by two men from a whaler, and it spread at an alarming rate, killing virtually every native who caught it. The primary reason for the shocking high mortality rate was not the measles itself, but the pneumonia which almost inevitably followed. When an Eskimo came down with the rash, and was beset with itching and high fever, his natural reaction was to strip down and run out into the cold to roll in the snow. Brevig's account of the number of sick and dead from this epidemic in his area alone is almost unbelievable—he and Mrs. Brevig nursed about seventy-five of the desperately ill around the clock, and buried the dead themselves. They all suffered from a severe shortage of food because there were too few men in shape to go out and hunt. Perhaps the most heart-breaking result of the epidemic was the large number of children left homeless by the death of parents and relatives. The Brevigs opened their home to all of the little ones, and this was the start of a Teller orphanage.

These efforts to help the stricken community were costly for the small mission. Brevig, while careful not to promote begging by asking for service or labor in exchange, had to give the villagers over $8,000 in supplies. He borrowed money and goods from the Alaska Commercial Company, when assured by the local government officials that Congress would come to his aid. Congress refused to appropriate anything to help the epidemic-stricken people, but instead passed on $75,000 for the building of a marine hospital along the Yukon River, where no marines were even stationed. Nothing could have been more ludicrous! Fortunately, however, one clause in the act stated that U. S. Revenue Commander David Jarvis (who had led the reindeer herd to Barrow) could use the money according to his best discretion. Thanks to David Jarvis, the debt incurred by Brevig to help the people was paid off.

Brevig remained at the Teller mission until 1917, and although he tried to retire three different times, he simply couldn't stay away from his long-time Eskimo friends, and the work he had begun among them. The Teller mission continues to this day, as do other missions started by Brevig during his travels about the Seward Peninsula—at Shishmaref and Igloo. They are a fitting memorial to a man who so loved and was loved by the Eskimos. As one of the Teller natives put it "He came and helped us when we were sick, and gave us food when he had nothing to eat, even while we were contrary to the God of whom he taught."[2]

---

2. Unpublished history of the Lutheran Eskimo Missions in Alaska, prepared by Luther Abrahamson, p. 5.

Both reindeer and gold played a part in the development of the Swedish Covenant mission at Unalakleet, an Eskimo village on the Bering Sea just south of Teller and the Seward Peninsula. Although this work was started by the Covenant of Sweden in 1887, it was turned over to the Swedish Evangelical Mission Covenant Church of America two years later.

The first two Swedish Covenant missionaries, Adolph Lydell (mentioned earlier as a founder of the Yakutat mission in Southeast Alaska) and Axel Karlson, had an international background in their lives and work. The two lived in the Caucasus region of Russia for a time, and Karlson was banished to Siberia, where he remained a prisoner for three years.

By then well versed in the Russian language, the pair spent a year in San Francisco learning English, and in the summer of 1887, went north to start mission work in Alaska. According to Swedish Covenant history, neither man had a specific area in mind—Lydell liked the beauty of the Yakutat Bay area and decided to remain there, while Karlson went on to St. Michael, on the Bering Sea coast. There he met Nashalook, an outstanding leader of the Eskimos at Unalakleet. The two could converse together in English and Russian, much to their mutual surprise and pleasure, and Nashalook invited the missionary back to live and work in his village.

Karlson's life in Unalakleet that first year was similar to that of the other early missionaries—he built himself a log house in which he taught school and held worship services, and he traveled extensively by dog team to many of the villages in the area. The one difference was that he preached his first sermons in Russian! The mission grew rapidly after that first year, and other Covenant missionaries, with medical and teaching training, then joined Karlson.

Although Unalakleet never experienced a gold rush stampede such as hit the beaches of Nome a few years later, great numbers of prospectors passed through the village and some gold was found in the area. The involvement of the Unalakleet mission in this part of the history of the Bering Sea coast is a highly controversial one—some missionaries took part in the gold stampede, while others made fortunes through help to gold seekers. Much of this money was used to further mission and church activities. As a Covenant leader recently put it:

"Picture a missionary staff with pitifully inadequate funds to do the things they dreamed of: to build schools, hospitals, churches, and orphanages for the people to whom they preached the message of God's love . . . one can then understand, though not excuse the missionaries and Covenant leaders for their interest in the Alaska gold, which our early involvement in Alaska's history, put them in a position to obtain." [3]

As the finding of gold influenced the lives of the people in the Unalakleet area, so did the introduction of reindeer. The small herds first given by Sheldon Jackson to the Unalakleet and nearby Golovin (also Covenant) missions increased rapidly. At one time each mission was supervising the care of over six thousand animals. These numbers decreased rapidly in later years, as did the herds in all other areas.

While reindeer helped supplement the food supply of the Unalakleet Eskimos, so did the gardens introduced by one of the later missionaries, E. B. Larsson. The earliest Covenant people grew a few potatoes and some root vegetables, but farming was a totally new idea to the rest of the populace. Described as the "Swedish garden parson," [4] Larsson distributed the seeds, the know-how, and the zeal all about the village. Before long, each cabin was surrounded by a neatly-tended garden, filled with carrots, beets, lettuce, cabbages and rhubarb. Things grew well in that soil, despite the short summer season, and although gardening declined after Larsson's departure, the Unalakleet area is still considered a garden spot of the north.

Over the years the Unalakleet mission was run by many other dedicated and hard-working men and women like E. B. Larsson. It is hard to single out any one person, but Ruth Ost, whose husband, L. E. Ost, spent fifty-one years in Alaskan mission service, was a truly remarkable woman in many ways. She served as a missionary herself for forty-two years, most of the time in severe pain from crippling arthritis. As her handicap grew progressively worse, she went from crutches to a wheel chair, and when she was unable to propel herself with her hands, she used toes and elbows.

---

3. Covenant Missions in Alaska, Arden Almquist, Covenant Press, Chicago, 1962, p. 23.
4. Covenant Missions in Alaska, Almquist; p. 44.

However, her affliction in no way curtailed her activities—to say the least: she was matron of the children's home for many years, school teacher, musician, Sunday School director, store-keeper, postmistress, midwife, and mother of eight children! Although she had no "specialty," she was highly regarded as a midwife, and only lost one baby in twenty-five years. After Ruth Ost's death in 1953, the Executive Secretary of Covenant World Missions said, "Her wheelchair was an altar, where those who came found salvation, restoration, healing and comfort."[5]

Probably the two most obvious results of the Covenant work at Unalakleet have been the large number of able and active Eskimo Christian leaders, and the education work carried on over the many years to the present. By 1905, the day and boarding schools at Unalakleet, Golovin and Yakutat had an enrollment of two hundred and eighty five pupils—a high figure in view of the small population of the three villages. After the government took over the elementary schools in 1927, the Covenant leaders concentrated on an industrial school for fifty boarding pupils at nearby White Mountain, and more recently, the Covenant high school at Unalakleet, which continues to this day. This school fills a great need along the northern coast, where there are virtually no high school facilities. In 1959, out of a total enrollment of forty-three students, eight seniors were accepted at the University of Alaska.

Many of the geographical names along the Bering Sea and Arctic coast are of English origin, thanks to explorers Captain Cook and Captain Beechey, and a few are strictly Eskimo such as Unalakleet and Kivalina. The name of the most famous gold rush town in Alaska is a mixture of the two—Nome. The story goes that when the first whalers landed at that part of the Seward Peninsula and attempted to speak with the natives, they invariably heard the words "No-me" or "Ki-no-me." In Eskimo, they mean "No" or "I don't know." The visitors assumed "No-me' was the name of the area. Many of the gold miners used this word for their camp near Anvil Creek (it was called Anvil City for a while) and it was quickly shortened to Nome.

---

5. Covenant Missions in Alaska, Almquist; p. 77.

Another story is told about the derivation of the name "Nome," and the residents of that city apparently accept both, without choosing between them. An old English chart of this northwest coast placed opposite the present-day Nome Cape, the word "Name" meaning that the cape was still unnamed. When this chart was later copied, the copyist misunderstood the meaning, and wrote "Nome." The gold mining town then took its name from Cape Nome.

Late in the fall of 1898, three prospectors found gold along Anvil Creek. Just a few months later, in mid-winter, quantities of the magic mineral were found among the sands of the shoreline there. Not only was this Seward Peninsula area much more accessible to Americans than the Klondike, but also the gold was readily available on the beach and along the streams.

So Nome became the goal of all gold seekers at the turn of the century, and, in one way, this was a big "break" for Alaska. The gold fever kindled a tremendous revival of interest in all of Alaska's resources, eventually bringing new harbors, docks, roads and railroads to help get the riches out. For the first time, also, Alaska was brought to the attention of millions of Americans—through gold rush stories in newspapers, magazines, and books written by Jack London, Rex Beach and others.

Nome and the Seward Peninsula also brought new wealth to the nation. In 1899 almost three million dollars in gold was found there, and in 1900 the figure went over four million, remaining at that for each of the next six years. (Twenty years of mining in Southeast Alaska, from 1880 to 1900, principally at the Juneau-Douglas mines, yielded about seventeen million dollars.)

Because the first news of gold found at Nome came in mid-winter, boats would have to wait until spring, and the stampede began in the Alaskan interior. Discouraged and disillusioned miners from the Klondike and other northern mining areas made haste to reach Nome by the overland Yukon river route before the hordes from the lower States could descend in the spring.

Roadhouses sprang up all along the river from Dawson to Kaltag, at intervals of twenty or twenty-five miles, so that the men could find stopping places each night. Prices skyrocketed overnight, and since most men traveled by dog team, the cost of a single sled dog went to over three hundred dollars. By late spring, the trail was so smooth and well-stamped out, that some men even made the whole journey on bicycles!

That winter, Episcopal Bishop Peter Rowe decided to send the Reverend Jules Prevost along with those gold seekers, in order to have some sort of church ready at Nome before the summer onslaught. Prevost made the six hundred mile journey from Tanana in forty-three days, and his first sight of Nome must have been something to be remembered. Nothing, other than gold, could have caused the building of a city on that spot. There was no harbor or roadstead, no shelter or protection of any kind and yet Nome became the perfect example of how men of the north could conquer local conditions and bring comfort amid the bleakness and desolation of nature.

When Prevost first arrived, he found a few cabins made from drift logs, and a number of tents. A snug little log cabin was the deputy recorder's office, one adjoining tent was a restaurant and barber shop, while another was the store of the Alaska Commercial Company. The most colorful tent was made of blue and white stripes, and housed the inevitable bar. The Episcopal priest lost no time in buying lots and setting up a tent church.

Bishop Rowe himself, was among the many thousands who came by boat in the summer of 1900, and he helped Prevost build a permanent wooden structure, the first actual church to be erected in Nome. It was closed a few years later, when the population declined. In his stories about the early worship services held there, the Bishop tells that in order to avoid the two feet of mud on the street and "sidewalk" he laid down several stout wooden planks leading to the church doorway. At the end of the service he discovered they had been stolen—wood was that precious a commodity in Nome at that time!

The Congregationalists, represented by a Dr. Wirth, arrived shortly after Jules Prevost, in the summer of 1899. They saw the great need for a hospital, and built one immediately. Their church building was begun in 1901, and I believe the same structure is still used today. Other denominations to come in at the beginning of the gold rush were the Catholics, who also built a hospital (mentioned earlier), and Presbyterian missionary S. Hall Young, active for so long in Southeast Alaska. After nine years of work in the lower States, he had decided to return with the gold seekers to the Klondike. He was fifty years old then, but held his own facing the physical rigors of the trail. When the Yukon gold rush simmered down, and Canadian ministers came in to care for the needs of the men, Young decided to move on to Nome.

He arrived by ship, and was virtually dumped ashore in the mad rush of thousands trying to land on an unprotected beach in small boats. His dinghy was actually swamped in the surf and his belongings lost, so he stepped ashore with no money and only wet clothes on his back. He was unsure just how to go about finding lodging and paying for meals, much less starting a mission, when he ran into a young couple who wanted to get married, and would pay him a twenty-five dollar fee. His work had begun!

That summer, at least one third of the men in Nome came down with typhoid fever, and Young was one of them. He was desperately ill for many weeks, and only survived because of the tremendous kindness, and twenty-four hour nursing care of a rough, tough saloon keeper. The man did everything he could to save the minister's life, even searching out daily fresh milk, a rarity in Nome at that time. Young later wrote that he had gained much insight from this experience and from his two years among the miners. He said that for the first time in his life, he was aware of the real richness and goodness latent in the hearts of even the roughest element of society.[6]

Once Young had recovered, he began holding services in a tent, but when the great influx of miners was over, the Presbyterians turned their work over to the Congregationalists. The Methodists, who had begun a church in Nome in 1906, also federated with the Congregationalists. However, they continued with mission work among the Nome natives, including a medical clinic, which later became Nome's Maynard McDougall Memorial Hospital.

---

6. Hall Young of Alaska, autobiography, p. 394.

Chapter VI

SOUTHCENTRAL ALASKA — CHILDREN'S HOMES AND MORAVIANS ALONG THE KUSKOKWIM

One of the earliest and largest of the mission boarding schools, and one which continues to this day, is the Jesse Lee Home, founded by the Woman's Missionary Society of the Methodist Church, at Unalaska, in the Aleutian Islands. Methodist women led the way for their denomination, creating a Bureau for Alaska in 1885. A year later, the Methodist Church sent the Reverend and Mrs. John Carr to Unga, in the Aleutian Chain to establish a church and school. Unfortunately, Mrs. Carr died within a year there, and her husband returned to the States.

The Methodist Church then discontinued their work at Unga—the Methodist mission policy was to concentrate on building churches in areas where a church could become self-supporting. Also, the Church felt its first responsibility was to the hordes of men seeking gold. So, attention was switched to early Southeastern boom towns. In 1897, the Reverend C. L. Larson was sent to Dyea, just north of Skagway, and he built the first Methodist church in the territory. Once the gold rush boom was over, however, the church was closed. A church begun in Skagway met the the same fate, and others begun in Fairbanks and Douglas were discontinued, but begun again in recent times. (The Methodist Church in Nome, begun in 1906, and federated with the Congregationalists in 1913, was separated and reactivated in 1948.)

The Methodist women, however, were vitally interested in educational, medical and social service programs for the Alaskan natives, and their societies all over the United States began raising money to support a children's home in the Territory. Dr. Jackson, while General Agent for Education, helped the women secure a 160-acre site at Unalaska, and the Jesse Lee Home (named for a man in the States who was one of the largest contributors), was established there in 1890.

Among the first of the missionaries to go to Unalaska was Miss Agnes Louise Sowle, who went alone in 1895. After three years of carrying on a "man-sized" job by herself, she returned to the States to marry her childhood sweetheart, Albert Newhall. When he had completed his medical education, they returned to the Jessie Lee Home, and devoted the rest of their lives to work among the Aleuts of Unalaska. "Mama" Newhall suffered a stroke while visiting in the States in 1915, but made her husband take her back to the Home. She died there and was buried beside two of her infant children in the little graveyard.

Mary Winchell, one of the women missionaries who helped the Newhalls run the Home, wrote a fascinating and lively account of daily living at an orphanage, in one of the most bleak and inaccessible parts of the world.[1] The men, women, and children at the Home had to spend much of their time and energies assuring themselves of a good local food supply, (imported goods being expensive and coming infrequently) so Miss Winchell's book is filled with delightful stories of these efforts.

Fish, of course, played an all-important role in their diet, and each summer all of the boys at the Home spent several weeks at a sheltered cove about eight miles away, setting nets and catching enough salmon to feed all the seventy children and their teachers for the rest of the winter. The women and girls either canned the fish, or salted it away in barrels so that it would last for many months.

It is astounding how effectively these early Alaskans could preserve food for such long periods in the days before freezers. On the other hand, the people of the North actually had plenty of "built-in" freezer room, thanks to the permafrost (ground perpetually frozen to a great depth and found throughout most of Central and Northern Alaska). Another Methodist mission home at Sinuk, near Nome, in its report one year, told of a large whale being washed ashore on their beach. The missionaries and villagers immediately buried it deep in the ground, and were able to use it for dog food all winter. The report also

---

1. Home by the Bering Sea, Mary E. Winchell, The Caxton Printers, Caldwell, Idaho, 1951.

mentioned the storage system used by the natives for berries, an all-important part of their diet. The villagers made bags out of seal skins, filled them with berries and hid them in caves in the frozen ground.

Berry-picking was an all-important activity at the Jesse Lee Home. It was also one the children loved, and the usual question of how much went into the stomach was just as applicable, there. Miss Winchell tells of spring outings when the children enjoyed hunting for red winter berries that grew close to the ground. The grownups felt they had no taste, but the little ones popped them in like candy, and took a few home to roast on top of the stove. An obnoxious odor usually "smelled up" the house, said Miss Winchell, but it wasn't anything compared to when the kids cooked the mussels they had found along the beach.

After months of a fairly monotonous diet of local food one can imagine the excitement at the Home when a boat brought in gifts of popcorn or candy. One of the most memorable treats of all was the Vermont maple sugar carried back by one of the women missionaries. None of the children had ever tasted it before, and it had been a long while for the grownups. Everyone gathered for the feast, melting the maple sugar cakes in a big iron kettle, and pouring it over dishes of packed snow—delicious!

At one time, the Mission thought it would be wonderful to have goat's milk for the children—the missionaries had all read about goats loving to climb mountains, eat grass and give quantities of milk. Unalaska had lots of mountains and plenty of grass, so it was decided to give it a try. A Methodist church in New Jersey heard about the request and sent up a big brown billy, named Frederick, a pretty white nanny named Adelaide (the names belonging to two of the most generous contributors) and two kids which the children promptly nicknamed Squig and Squirm.

And then the trouble began. The goats did not want to climb the mountains or eat the grass. They preferred to wander downtown, onto the docks, into the school house and the general store. They even got themselves into the local Russian

Orthodox Church, into one room which was considered so sacred that only priests were allowed to enter. The goats just didn't understand. After all, they had been advertised as being friendly and enjoying the company of people!

Dr. Newhall tried staking the animals, but they simply pulled up the sticks and the mission house then became the main target of their visits. The dining room was their favorite haunt, eating the sugar from the sugar bowl, often pulling off the whole table cloth just to get at the delicacy. They were usually chased away with brooms, until one day it was discovered that the goats had chewed the stems off all the brooms. The dining room wasn't the only place so honored by these visits—daily chapel gatherings were frequently interrupted by the bleating of goats at the doorway—wanting human company. And, they loved to climb the fire escapes, to look into second floor bedrooms, and to go up onto the roof, where the shingles were delicious!

The crowning blow for Miss Winchell came the day she placed all of her precious potted plants in the chapel for a funeral service. When she went back to collect them, she found nothing left but dirt. There's no need to explain how it happened. Actually, the crowning blow to the entire goat episode was the discovery that the nanny did not give quantities of milk. In fact, Adelaide never gave more than a pint at a single milking—barely enough for the one mission baby, who preferred the Carnation variety, anyway. Needless to say, there were few tears shed when Frederick died from some mysterious malady, and on the Thanksgiving after the goats' arrival, the mission dined on the most sumptous meal—you guessed it—roast goat!

Mary Winchell had just as many trials and tribulations with chickens as with goats. Before she returned from one of her vacations to the States, Dr. Newhall asked her to buy a dozen chickens in Seattle and bring them back to the mission with her. The hardships of travel to and from Alaska in those days were enough, without including animals to look after, too. Miss Winchell had to go down to the hold to clean the cages daily, and collect whatever chickweed and grasses she could find at each stop, to keep them well-fed. Once the ship reached Seward, Mary transferred to a small boat, so the chicken crates had to be lashed to the deck. On the stormy run to the Aleutians, it was a wonder that the chickens ever survived the constant ducking from waves which washed over the little craft.

To make matters more difficult, the Captain told her a series of stories about other chickens traveling with missionaries. It seems that some traveling to Nome had the great misfortune of being ferried ashore to the Nome beach in a small boat which overturned. Those birds drowned in the surf. Another missionary doctor frequently visited his feathered charges in the hold of a larger ship, and noticed at the start of the voyage, that a couple of hound dogs were tethered there, too. Just before they reached their destination, he was told the inevitable—the hound dogs had broken loose and devoured every one of the chickens. Miss Winchell did not have to worry about the surf, as Unalaska had a dock, and there were no dogs aboard her ship, so her chickens arrived safely!

In 1925, mainly because of travel and climate problems, the Jessie Lee Home was moved to Seward, where it carried on the same kind of boarding school home, and after the 1964 earthquake, it was moved to new quarters in Anchorage. The Methodist women also supported the Sinuk mission home, mentioned earlier, and in 1913, established the Lavinia Wallace Young Mission in Nome. This mission was not a boarding school, like the others, but a place where the natives of Nome could go for help, instruction, for social activities, and medical aid.

Again, it was the churchwomen who took the initiative for the American Baptists. In 1893, the Woman's American Baptist Home Mission Society appointed Professor and Mrs. W. E. Roscoe as Alaskan missionaries, and funds were provided to buy land and build a children's home on Woody Island, just one mile from Kodiak. The island has been described as one of the most beautiful spots in Alaska—covered with hemlock and spruce trees, with high hills and white sand beaches. The two dormitories were built near a small lake, which could be used for skating in winter and boating during the warm months. The climate and soil were good for farming, so the mission was able to raise much of its own food. An early Kodiak newspaper account mentions "cattle in the meadows, horses at work pulling the plow or hauling hay, chickens about the stables, ducks and geese on the lake."[2] — reminding one of a farm anywhere in the lower States!

The first child was taken into the Mission Home in July of 1893, and from that moment on, the two buildings housed an average of seventy children at one time. Some of the youngsters, ranging in age from two to seventeen, were orphans, but many came from homes broken by illness or disaffection. A mission pamphlet tells a typical story of the arrival of some of the children. An Aleut father appeared at the Home with three little ones in tow—"How do, Mr. Superintendent! My wife gone. My children's have no one to care for them, but me. Come time now I must go fish for cannery . . . I spend all money for Mary when she sick. I cannot buy food. I cannot get someone take care of children. I see many children here, all happy and well. My children poor, ragged, hungry."[3]

The children at the home were given much more than food, clothing, and a Christian upbringing. Their activities were many and varied, including attending a government school right at the mission. Medical care was also always available, because one of the missionaries was also a doctor. The girls learned sewing and cooking and helped in the gardens (also making forty pounds of butter a week!), while the boys did most of the farming, and even raised money by catching enough salmon and codfish to feed the mission and sell locally.

The best description of life for the children in the Home comes from one of the youngsters, and was printed in a Primary Graded Bible Leaflet: "There is work to do, of course. The girls clean and dust. They help prepare the meals. They wash and dry the dishes. The boys make their own beds. They brings wood for the fire. They milk the cows . . . Each child has a garden where he raises flowers and vegetables. They have good times playing together, too. There is a playroom in each home. Here the children keep their games and toys. In

---

2. Early Kodiak newspaper, courtesy of The Kodiak Baptist Mission.
3. Mission pamphlet, courtesy of The Kodiak Baptist Mission.

North American Commercial Company's wharf at Dutch Harbor, Unalaska Bay, 1893.

(Courtesy Presbyterian Board of National Missions)

Girls' House, Jesse Lee Home, Unalaska, Alaska, around 1910. The Boys' House is in the background.

(Reprinted with permission of the Caxton Printers and Mary Winchell. Photo from "Home by the Bering Sea," Mary Winchell)

Mary Winchell reading to a group of children in her room at the Jesse Lee Home, around 1910.

The girls' sewing class takes a recess break—The Jesse Lee Home, around 1910.

(Reprinted with permission of the Caxton Printers and Mary Winchell. Photos from "Home by the Bering Sea," Mary Winchell)

Three of the younger Jesse Lee Home residents—around 1910.
(Reprinted with permission of the Caxton Printers and Mary Winchell.
Photo from "Home by the Bering Sea," Mary Winchell)

The Chapel and Baptist Home on Woody Island—before 1910.

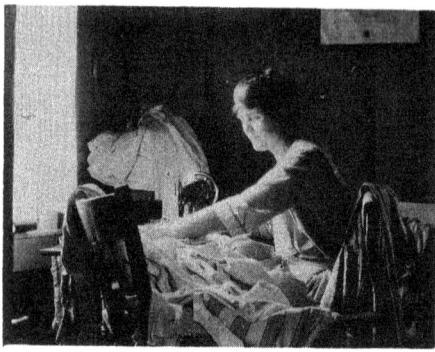

Mending day at the Baptist Children's Home. The lady beneath the mounds of clothing is Goldie Bailey—around 1900.

The Kodiak Baptist Home at its new location on Kodiak —1926.

(Courtesy of The Kodiak Baptist Mission)

the winter, they go skating and sledding. In the summer they have picnics and the boys and girls wade and swim in the lake." [4]

The Kodiak Children's Home continues to this day, as a part of the Kodiak Baptist Mission. After a disastrous fire in 1937, the location was moved across the channel, to Kodiak Island itself. Three buildings were constructed, each to act as a home for ten to fourteen children. The farm was enlarged to such an extent that twenty-five head of Herefords supply most of the meat for the home, and chickens are laying some ten thousand eggs in two years out of three. The fishing is just as good—the mission boys caught three tons of salmon in one afternoon a few years ago, and some of it is still in tins on the shelves at the Home.

At the same time that the home was rebuilt, another identical cottage was erected at nearby Ouzinkie which served as both a children's Home and a village Christian Center. Ouzinkie became the home port for the mission boat "Evangel." which ministered to remote villages around the Island of Kodiak, establishing Sunday Schools and holding worship services.

As the Baptists had agreed with Sheldon Jackson to take on work in Southcentral, Alaska, so the Moravians accepted the call for missions in the Kuskokwim Valley. In 1883, Dr. Jackson met with leaders of the Moravian Church at Bethlehem, Pennsylvania, and told them of the pitiful conditions among the Eskimos of that region. In 1884, the Moravian Church sent the Reverend Henry Hartman and William Weinland on a long survey journey throughout the Bristol Bay and Lower Kuskokwim districts. They found only two missions in the entire area—both Russian Orthodox—at Nushagak and Kolamakofski. So, in 1885, William Weinland, John Kilbuck, their wives, and lay member Hans Torgersen were sent to establish a Moravian mission at Bethel. Torgersen was drowned during his first year there. Kilbuck, who was a full-blooded Delaware Indian, worked at Bethel until his death in 1922.

---

4. Primary Graded Bible Leaflet, W. P. Shelton, published by the Judson Press, Seattle Washington, 1941, p 2

Within the next few years, a number of other Moravian missions were set up in the Kuskokwim region, and more missionaries came in to help carry on the expanded work. Dr. Joseph Romig was one of this later group, coming in 1896. The brother of Mrs. Kilbuck, Romig knew when very young, just what he was going to do and where he was headed. The Moravian Church provided for his medical education, and supplied him with instruments and drugs for his work in the north. He very wisely supplied himself with an equally dedicated wife who was a nurse!

After joining the Kilbucks at Bethel, Dr. Romig plunged right into medical practice, traveling almost constantly throughout the large Kuskokwim area to care for the numerous sick and afflicted. He felt that the Eskimos were originally an extraordinarily healthy people, with good teeth, and few of the outsider's diseases, such as cancer, diabetes, or scurvey. The trouble began when the visitor brought in his diseases, liquor, white bread, and cotton clothing, and also drove the game and fish away.

Romig was appalled by the high infant mortality rates— so many babies died before reaching one year of age that Eskimo women had learned not to lavish any affection on a new baby; too much heartbreak was likely to be the result. The new-born were wrapped in rabbit skins and then virtually abandoned. If they survived the first twenty-four hours, they were then given nourishment, but still no love or attention. It's amazing that any Eskimos lived to grow up at that time!

It was obvious to Romig, and to Kilbuck, who had pleaded for a doctor to join him, how much good for the Church a medical missionary could do. An incident involving an insane chieftain had greatly damaged the prestige of the Bethel mission before Romig's arrival —Kilbuck had been blamed for the insanity, and for inability to cure the man. Doctor Romig's skill quickly overcame this hostility, and in a most dramatic way. The brother of this same chieftain put a harpoon through his hand, and, whereas the Eskimos usually died from such an injury, Romig was able to heal the wound.

A short time later, Kilbuck himself developed blood poisoning in an arm (from a fish hook in his finger) and this condition always meant death to the Eskimos at that time. The Doctor operated, allowing some of the natives to watch, amputated the arm, and Kilbuck recovered — much to the amazement of the local population.

All went well for the little mission until the fall of 1899. The last regular trading boat was unable to leave winter provisions, so the families faced the long winter with virtually nothing on their shelves. Confronted with total starvation, Romig and another man took two large skin boats up to the Yukon, and St. Michael. Barely surviving an extremely difficult journey, they were able to bring back enough supplies to keep themselves going until spring.

Another crisis of much greater proportion hit the entire community during the summer of 1900 — the same measles epidemic which had wreaked havoc along the Bering Sea and Arctic Coasts. The disease was brought into the Bethel area by a trading ship, which was also bringing in the first coffins the natives had ever seen. The Eskimos all concluded that the coffins were the evil omen which brought the disease.

There were seventy-two deaths at the Bethel mission alone, and of the three thousand five hundred natives who lived in the area, over one thousand five hundred died that summer. The winter which followed was a tragic and difficult one for everybody because so few people had been able to hunt and fish during the summer months — a story familiar to the Teller mission on the coast, and to many others that year as well.

One of Dr. Romig's innumerable medical missions involved a trip to Holy Cross. Father Robout was at that Catholic mission then, and was suffering from blood poisoning as the result of a frozen toe. The Doctor was able to save him by amputating the foot. While staying at the mission, he could observe the Catholic work there, and was tremendously impressed with what these missionaries were accomplishing. This was the start of a deep friendship (especially with Bishop Crimont, who was in charge then) which carried on for many years. Romig was later a surgeon in three Catholic hospitals. When the Doctor pleaded for a better hospital facility in the rapidly growing town of Anchorage, Bishop Crimont exerted great influence to have $500,000 allocated for such a purpose.

Dr. Romig's work was not all medical — after long days of treating patients, he spent his evenings telling Bible stories to any Eskimo listeners he could find. If we sometimes find it difficult to interpret and understand the Bible parables, one can easily understand the translating problem facing Romig. He was particularly stymied by the parable of the sowers — how could he get this across to a people who had never sowed seed or seen grain? The Doctor finally substituted the far more familiar berries. The message "in my Father's house are many mansions," also posed problems — how could he make heaven desirable in terms of igloos? He settled this one by showing the Eskimos pictures of the buildings in Seattle and it worked! When it came time to tell the Christmas story, Romig, and undoubtedly most other missionaries, substituted caribou for camels, reindeer for sheep, and the northern lights for the Christmas Star.

In later years, the Romig family moved to other parts of Alaska — contributing much to the development of the territory. Romig was a cannery doctor at Nushagak for a few years, and while there, made a strong appeal for a better legal system. At that time law-breaking cannery workers had to go all the way to Valdez to a Court. Because of his plea, in 1909, U. S. Revenue Cutters became floating courtrooms for the many isolated areas along the Coast.

The doctor was also instrumental in getting the first U.S. mail contract from Bethel to Holy Cross—he was appointed U.S. Commissioner for two years, and in 1909, the U.S. Bureau of Education appointed him Superintendent and Physician to Southwestern Alaska. He later joined hospitals in Seward, Fairbanks and Anchorage, and some of his family still live in Anchorage today.

Chapter VII

ALASKAN CHURCHES FACE NEW CHALLENGES

In his history of Alaska Senator Gruening wrote ". . . much of the progress in assimilating the native to the white culture was due to the early missionary effort transformed in part after 1884 into a federally conducted educational system, which, despite its chronic insufficiency of appropriations, represented till the end of the century the only evidence of governmental interest in the people of Alaska." [1]

The gigantic task of bringing education to all of the widely scattered and culturally divergent peoples of the vast Alaskan territory was too large for the little group of dedicated missionaries and their equally small financial resources. Out of an estimated school population of almost ten thousand in 1894, only one thousand four hundred and thirty-eight were enrolled in the twenty-four schools (officially recognized by the federal government) operating in Alaska, according to the figures of Clarence Hulley.[2] After 1894 the Federal government withdrew subsidies from mission schools, and although some continued to operate under denominations who used their own financing, twenty of the schools were placed under the direct control of agents of the Bureau of Education, under the Department of the Interior. From then on, education in the Eskimo and Indian villages remained a separate system, eventually placed under the control of the Bureau of Indian Affairs.

In the meantime, the rapidly increasing Causcasian population in Alaska was becoming less transient, and "raising cane" over the lack of proper schooling for their children. In 1890 Congress passed an act providing for the incorporation of towns and establishing, within these towns, "schools for white children under the control of locally-elected school boards." [3] All funds for upkeep were to come from local sources.

---
1. The State of Alaska, Ernest Gruening, p. 359
2. Alaska, Past and Present, Clarence Hulley, p. 243
3. Alaska, Past and Present, Clarence Hulley, p. 243

This first step toward a territorial school system still ignored the non-native children living in unincorporated rural areas. In 1905 Congress passed the Nelson act which provided for schools for these children, under the supervision of the territorial governor, and operated with funds obtained from liquor and trade licenses issued outside incorporated towns. It really wasn't until 1917, fifty years after the purchase of Alaska, that Congress granted the territorial legislature full power to establish a uniform school system for all but the native villages.

So, although the missions in the territory withdrew from the field of public education when the governments began to take on their proper function, some mission schools remained active and carry on to this day. In Southeast Alaska the Sheldon Jackson Junior College, founded by the earliest Presbyterian mission leaders, continues to play a major role in the state's higher education. Still situated in Sitka on the original three hundred and fifty four acre grant obtained from Congress, most of the campus buildings, including a swimming pool, have been added recently. The complex includes a five year boarding high school as well as the two year fully accredited junior college, and students of all races come from throughout Alaska and other states to obtain a high level education. (In 1965 the total enrollment for both schools was two hundred and twenty-five.)

While the buildings and curriculum are modern and up-to-date, the Sheldon Jackson museum, on one corner of the campus sharply reminds the visitor of the school's colorful past. The octagonal building was put up by Jackson himself. Said to be the first concrete structure in Alaska, Jackson was called "the man who can make stone" by local Indians when he concocted a gravel and cement mixture to form the walls. The museum itself contains Alaskan artifacts gathered by Jackson during his many travels about Alaska.

In the northern and central areas of Alaska, among other mission schools which remain active are the Covenant High School at Unalakleet, also supported by the Friends, the Jesse Lee Methodist children's home which recently moved to Anchorage, and the American Baptist children's home on Kodiak. This same denomination opened another home for youngsters in need of a temporary place to stay, in Anchorage in 1965, built with gifts of money sent in after the 1964 earthquake.

The Catholic Church continues to play an active role in education in Alaska, maintaining boarding schools at Holy Cross, St. Mary's, Nulato and Copper Valley missions, and day schools at Juneau, Ketchikan, Fairbanks and Anchorage (one is planned for Kodiak). Some are still run by the Jesuit order and others are under the direction of the dioceses of Juneau and Fairbanks and the Archdiocese of Anchorage. (A tremendous boast to Catholic work in Alaska was the creation by the Pope in 1965, of this Archdiocese at Anchorage).

The most recent major addition to denominational education was the Alaska Methodist University, an accredited liberal arts college which began operation in Anchorage in 1960 under the presidency of Dr. Frederick P. McGinnis, former superintendent of Methodist work in Alaska. The only four year college in Alaska, other than the State's University of Alaska, it was built under the direction of the Methodist Division of National Missions on two hundred and forty-two acres purchased by citizens of Anchorage, and given to the University for a campus. The enrollment in 1966 was 577 students, coming from all parts of Alaska and other states. The most recently constructed campus building was designed by Edward Durell Stone, nationaly known architect, and is an appropriate symbol of the gigantic forward strides achieved by Alaskan education in recent years. An additional significant fact—the initial survey for this Alaska Methodist University was conducted by Doctor P. Gordon Gould, the first native Alaskan to become an ordained Methodist minister.

Church activity in the medical field also decreased with the awakening of concerned government officials. It was not until 1916 that the federal government initiated a native medical service in Alaska, and most of the denominational hospitals were either taken over by the government or the local communities. Medical facilities still run by Alaskan churches today include the Methodist Maynard MacDougall Hospital in Nome, the Cordova hospital, owned by the community, but administered by the American Baptists, and the five hospitals run by the Catholic Sisters of Providence in Ketchikan, Juneau, Fairbanks, Kodiak and Anchorage.

While the churches (other than Catholic) have switched their work emphasis from the public education and medical fields, there has been no lessening of activity. They have changed their emphasis to areas where efforts are more needed—a shift in activities to keep abreast with the rapid development of Alaska as a state. Although civilization has found its way into every far away corner of this largest new state, one of the greatest challenges still facing the modern missionaries is the conquest of the vast distances between the peoples under their care. Thanks to twentieth century technology, however, dog teams, canoes and steamboats have been largely relegated to the past. The radio, ships, cars, trains, planes, and even the snowmobile have taken over, and although the glamour of Gold Rush Alaska may be gone, another kind of equally challenging and adventurous ministry has taken its place.

The radio has developed into an effective means of reaching people in greatly isolated areas. The Evangelical Covenant Mission, with the cooperation of the Lutherans and Friends, built and staffed the 5,000 watt brodcast station KICY in Nome in 1960, with a range from Point Hope in the north to the Pribilof Islands in the south. While its basic aim is to proclaim the Christian gospel, it is done largely through programs of entertainment, news and music, with some preaching and religious teachings included. And, many of the programs are broadcast in Eskimo dialects.

In the Southeast, the Presbyterian Board of National Missions started radio station KSEW at Sitka in order to carry similar broadcasting to the homes in that area. Later taken over by a group of men and women of many denominations, the station has become a self-supporting "radio church." It also provides good training for students at nearby Sheldon Jackson Junior College. Dr. Walter Soboleff, well-known native Tlingit leader and Presybterian minister, frequently broadcasts sermons and lessons in the Tlingit language. At the opposite end of the state, in far-north Wainwright, Eskimo minister Roy Ahmoagak has found a unique way to broadcast Sunday night devotions to his villagers—he simply hitches his radio to an oscilator, and uses a small hand-held microphone!

Boats have been used by missionaries to get about ever since the earliest canoe travels of S. Hall Young. Catholic and Episcopal workers leaned heavily on the use of small boats to travel up and down rivers of the interior during the summer months. The Episcopal launch, "the Pelican" was first put into use at Fort Yukon in 1908, and it covered over 5,200 miles each summer for many years, carrying the missionaries to sprouting towns, widely-flung villages, and countless of native summer fishing camps. ("The Pelican" was later replaced by the launch "The Godspeed".) In Southeast Alaska, Presbyterians retired the canoe, and continue to visit the many isolated logging camps, canneries and little far-from-church villages with the ultra-modern motor vessel "Anna Jackman," named for the wife of Dr. A. Earl Jackman, head of Alaska Mission work for Presbyterians from 1944 to 1960.

In Southcentral Alaska, Presbyterians bring Christianity to equally isolated homesteaders, miners, and construction workers in a unique way—via the railroad. Sometimes called the "world's longest church", the 252 mile Railbelt Congregation between Fairbanks and Anchorage (the only railroad in Alaska) not only gets frequent "friendly visits" from pastors, but also Sunday School classes for children. The Reverend Bert Bingle was one of the first missionaries to take to the train, and he also took to the road, wearing out 14 cars in his many years of ministry along the Alaska Highway. The Bingles went from Cordova to the Matanuska Valley in 1934 when the U.S. Government sent 899 settlers there from the "dust bowl" to become farmers. His days were busy with helping unhappy people facing miserable and unfamiliar living conditions. Life gradually improved for those homesteaders who stuck it out, and Bert Bingle helped build the United Protestant Church at Palmer—also called the Church of a Thousand Trees because it took that many to do the job!

Perhaps the most familar of the many exciting and adventuresome stories of modern Alaska missionaries are about those who have taken to the airplane. After the arrival of the romantic and daring bush pilots in the mid 20's, the missionaries began taking to the air themselves—Bishop Rowe made his first flight in a commercial plane in 1927, covering the distance from Nome to Point Hope in one day instead of the usual three or four weeks by dog sled! It quickly became obvious that an airplane could be of tremendous service to Alaskan missions, and while some denominations chose to fly with commercial carriers, others were given or raised money for single engine planes, flown by the missionaries themselves, who either had learned to fly during World War II or just decided to take lessons on the spot. One of the most famous of this new breed of evangelists, was the Catholic "Glacier Priest", Father Bernard R. Hubbard, S. J. The Reverend Paul Carlson logged many hours for the Evangelical Covenant Mission, and the Reverend Bill Wartes, while living at Barrow, flew the Presbyterian Cessna between their Arctic missions.

One of this group who is still flying, year in and year out, almost daily among his far-flung missions and parishes, is Episcopal Bishop William J. Gordon, Jr. Bill Gordon first came to Seward as a Deacon, and then went north with his wife (whom he had met on the boat from Seattle) to Point Hope in 1943. During their four years there, their life was similar to that of the earlier missionaries—virtually cut off from the rest of the world—without mail for three or four months at a time, supplies brought in once a year, six months of dusk and darkness, and the weather as vicious as that which greeted Dr. Driggs many years before.

The Bishop began his ministry with a dogteam, following the first missionary's footsteps, and later, while living in Fairbanks, he logged over 10,000 miles by motor launch along the Tanana, Yukon and Koyukuk Rivers. So, Bishop Gordon was familiar with both the old and the new, and he decided that flying would be more economical than feeding eleven dogs or buying fuel for slow boats. He also knew that the time factor would be of great importance to his work. After four years at Point Hope, he was elected Episcopal Bishop of Alaska, the youngest in the history of his church, given responsibility for nineteen missions and twenty-one outstations over an area more than twice the size of Texas.

Once the Bishop had finished his flying lessons, he was off, and hasn't stopped since. Two of his planes (like the Reverend Bingle and his cars, he has worn out a few planes) have been called the "Blue Box," purchased with funds from Episcopal

The Present Campus of Sheldon Jackson Junior College, Sitka.

The Sheldon Jackson Museum, on the Campus of Sheldon Jackson Junior College, Sitka.
(Courtesy of the Presbyterian Board of National Missions.)

The new Student Union-Residence Complex at Alaska Methodist University. The building was designed by architect Edward Durell Stone.
(Courtesy of Alaska Methodist University, photograph by Jon Gardey.)

Anchorage's ultra-modern 150-bed Providence Hospital built in 1962 and run by the Sisters of Providence.
(Courtesy of Providence Hospital)

Dr. Walter Soboloff, Presbyterian Minister, broadcasts in Native Tlingit.

The Rev. Roy Ahmaogak broadcasts an evening devotional to the villagers of Wainwright.

(Courtesy of the Presbyterian Board of National Missions.)

The Reverend Milton Swan, Eskimo priest of the Episcopal Church at Kivalina.

(Courtesy of the Right Rev. William J. Gordon)

The Presbyterian Church at Anaktuvuk Pass, a village of 125 people in the Brooks Range, north of the Arctic Circle.

Presbyterian elder Elijah Kakinya at Anaktuvuk Pass.
(Courtesy of Presbyterian Board of National Missions.)

The College Community Church at the University of Alaska in Fairbanks.

(Photograph by Joseph M. Elkins; courtesy of the Presbyterian Board of National Missions.)

Trikes, low tables, swings, and the yard full of children show that churchly as the building still appears on the outside, Memorial Church, Juneau, is indeed what its sign says, a day care center.

(Courtesy of Presbyterian Board of National Missions.)

Anchorage's new First Baptist Church, due to be completed in April, 1967, with a total membership of 1200.
(Courtesy of the First Baptist Church)

The Salvation Army helps rescue workers after the great Alaska Earthquake.
(Courtesy of the Salvation Army)

At Point Hope in 1965, the 75th anniversary celebration of the founding of the Episcopal mission there. The villagers help celebrate with the traditional "blanket-toss."

Bishop William J. Gordon at Point Hope for the celebration, takes his turn at the "blanket-toss."

(Photos by the author)

Bishop William J. Gordon, the Reverend Milton Swan and Bishop John E. Hines, Presiding Bishop of the Protestant Episcopal Church of the United States, take part in the Point Hope celebration.

The Reverend Keith Lawton, in charge of the Point Hope mission in 1965, visits with an Eskimo parishioner.

(Photos by the author)

The Reverends David Salmon, Titus Peter and Isaac Tritt—1964.
(Courtesy of The Right Rev. William J. Gordon)

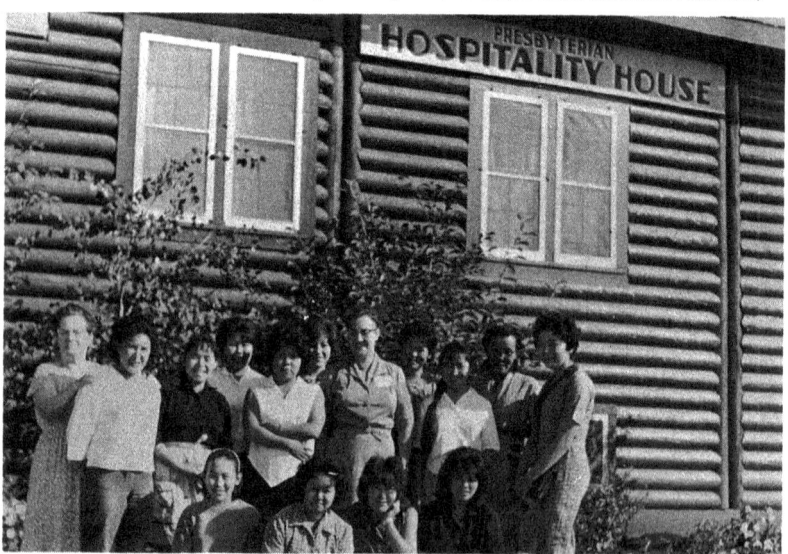

Lacquered log former American Legion Hall in Fairbanks shelters Presbyterian Hospitality House and its overflow family. Here part of the group gathers before going to jobs or beginning daily work details. Housekeeping director Vi Smith is at left and administrator Mabel Rasmussen is in midst of girls.
(Courtesy of the Presbyterian Board of National Missions)

Churchwomen's blue Thank Offering boxes. His travels average about 50,000 miles a year—with skiis in the winter and wheels in the summer, and no one will dispute the fact that he is undoubtedly familiar with every airfield, bush strip and sand bar in the far north.

Bishop Gordon, and leaders of other Alaskan denominations, are faced with a double ministry, just as that confronting Bishop Rowe at the turn of the century. But, the dual aspects of this ministry have changed with the changing times. The challenge before Bishop Rowe was that of helping the native villagers face the great transition from a primitive culture to a twentieth century society, and at the same time helping the newcomers, the transient gold seekers living in temporary camps, facing unaccustomed hardships and difficult conditions. One of the dual challanges facing the Church today is essentially unchanged—to continue to help the native peoples find their way into the twentieth century; but the ministry to the transient miners went out with the gold rush days, and has been replaced by the task of tackling the many problems evolving from a rapidly expanding, relatively sedentary urban society.

The village people of today can no longer earn a living off the land; the men (and some of the women) must seek outside employment, frequently in urban areas, and the children must go to towns and cities to obtain higher education. Their inner conflicts are great as the modern life they enter tears away their old cultural foundation. While these people now obtain public education and medical care from the government, they look to the Church for spiritual needs and community responsibility. (In many villages, the entire population belongs to one church, so that in a sense, the community is the church and the church the community.)

Because the Episcopal Church withdrew from administration of public education and hospitals, it has been able to maintain more mission stations, filling each with a resident priest. Bishop Gordon believes (as do many others in the mission field) that while in the earlier days the Church sought to meet the problems of the villagers by assigning one priest to several villages scattered over vast areas, visiting them only a few times a year, today they have learned that this is an inadequate ministry, that the Christian faith can be best taught by Christians who daily live the faith in the very midst of the people.

Many mission leaders feel that one way to bring a closer relationship between the Church and the village is to make a more concerted effort toward a native ministry. A number of leading Indian and Eskimo ministers have already been mentioned in earlier chapters. The Episcopal Church was slower than some other denominations in concentrating on this aspect of mission work. They now have three Indian priests, the Reverends Titus Peter, David Salmon and Isaac Tritt, and two deacons, Philip Peter and David Paul in the Yukon Valley area (in addition to Milton Swan, the Eskimo priest on the Arctic Coast).

With the growth of Alaska's towns and cities, requiring a new ministry to cope with the special problems of urban communities, the mushrooming population has also brought in many new denominations, so many that the latest list of all churches and denominations in Alaska covers eighteen pages! (Forty-nine churches and missions, with a total membership of 7,500 belong to the Alaska Baptist Convention alone. The Russian Orthodox Church claims ninety-six churches, with a membership of 20,000, but only nineteen ministers.) After looking at this formidable list, I would add one further new challenge facing these churches today: the Christian cause in Alaska can never become truly strong until all of these groups are brought into communication with each other, and eliminate the duplication of efforts and funds which radically weaken their ministry and lesson the impact upon the people.

In urban areas, most of the denominations have active programs for the town and city dweller, such as the Catholic Youth Organizations, the Presbyterian Day Care Center in Juneau, and the Presbyterian Hospitality House in Fairbanks. The latter is an urban home for girls from rural areas while they look for jobs or go to school. United Churchwomen in Anchorage plan to open a similar facility in the next year. In terms of such services in urban areas, the Salvation Army has been indispensible in many ways. In the city of Anchorage, with a population of about 60,000, but with no city welfare program of its own, the Salvation Army has played a vital role in help rendered to those in need--help through facilities such as a men's social center, vocational rehabilitation, family service bureau, and Booth Memorial Home for unwed mothers. In 1965 over 5,000 persons were aided, either with gifts of food and clothing or with professional help through one of these services.

Although the Salvation Army was a latecomer to Anchorage (1948), workers first came to Alaska, to Skagway, with the Klondike gold seekers of 1898. In fact, Evangeline Booth, daughter of the founder of the organization, was among those first Army pioneers. Work spread from that town to other Southeast communities, and continues there to this day.

By no means the least important of the Salvation Army's many local activities is aid in times of disaster. And no one organization did more than they for stricken Alaskan communities after the devastating earthquake of 1964. In Anchorage, within moments of the end of the shaking, forty trained Army workers were on the scene, ready to meet immediate needs, providing strong leadership and clear thinking, maintaining desks at Civilian Defense Headquarters. The Salvation Army building itself became the official clearing house for displaced persons, homeless families were provided with housing, food and clothing, and ten Salvation Army mobile units kept rescue workers fed with over 200 pounds of meat, 7,000 cookies and seventy-five cases of coffee! While earthquakes break up ground and buildings, they also tear into the composure of human lives—the assurance of a comforting "God bless you" from an "angel in blue" is also a most effective part of the selfless ministry of the Salvation Army.

I find it difficult to end a narrative such as this: to the many men and women helping to build Alaska today, it is the present and the future that count. In many ways they face the most tremendous challenge ever, and they face it with a courage, enthusiasm and perseverence which cannot be matched.

And yet, one must build on the foundations of the past, and the history of the missionary efforts in Alaska is a glorious one, perhaps unequalled anywhere. It is all too easy to look back and criticise some of the decisions, the efforts of these early Alaskans—this will always be a part of the story; but not the important part. It is what was achieved for Alaska and Alaskans, in the face of overwhelming odds, by these men and women who dedicated their lives to God. It is their stories which can help to sustain and encourage the workers of today and tomorrow, can be as the voice of one crying in the wilderness—"hear ye the voice of the Lord".

BIBLIOGRAPHY

A Bibliography of Alaskan Literature (1724-1824) Vol. I, Wickersham
History of Alaska, Bancroft
The State of Alaska, Gruening
Alaska, 1741-1963, Clarence Hully
A Story of Alaska, Clarence Andrews
Conditions in Alaska, Congressional Report—1904
Nome and Seward Peninsula, Harrison (1905)
Point Hope, by James W. VanStone
Monuments in Cedar—Edward Keithahn
Hall Young of Alaska (Autobiography)
Alaskan Apostle (Sheldon Jackson), Lazell
Report on Education in Alaska—1886, Jackson
Introduction of Domestic Reindeer—1901, 1904, Jackson
Pioneer Life in the Yukon Valley, Rev. James Kirk
Presbyterian Leadership in Pioneer Alaska, Hinckley
Haines Presbyterian Church Pamphlet (History of their missions in Chilkat Valley)
Letters of Amanda McFarland, Journal of the Presbyterian Historical Society
Life in Alaska, Letters of Mrs. Eugene S. Willard
History of Presbyterian Missions in Alaska, Luther M. Dimmit (Courtesy of the Presbyterian Board of National Missions)
Alaska Missionary, Drebert (Romig)
Dog Team Doctor, Eva Greenslit Anderson (Romig)
Apaurak in Alaska, Dr. Johnshoy (Brevig)
History of the Lutheran Eskimo Missions in Alaska, Luther Abrahamson
Covenant Missions in Alaska, Almquist
Raymond and I, Elizabeth Robins (early Nome)
Home by the Bering Sea, Mary Winchell
Methodism in Alaska and Hawaii, Middleton
The Man of Alaska, Thomas Jenkins (Bishop Rowe)
Metlakatla Christian Mission, pamphlet by William Duncan Memorial Church
The Apostle of Alaska, Arctander (William Duncan)
Peter Trimble Rowe, Mary Cox, pamphlet by Pioneer Builders for Christ
John Driggs among the Eskimos, pamphlet by Pioneer Builders for Christ
A Winter Circuit of Our Arctic Coast, Hudson Stuck

Alaska Missions of the Episcopal Church, Hudson Stuck
Ten Thousand Miles with a Dog Sled, Hudson Stuck
The Ascent of Denali, Hudson Stuck
Hudson Stuck of Alaska, pamphlet by Pioneer Builders for Christ
Catholic Builders of the Nation
The Catholic Encyclopedia
Catholic Letters:
1. A letter of Father Julius Jette to Very Rev. Father Rene, Nov. 14, 1898, The Woodstock Letters
2. The Woodstock Letters; Vol. XXXI, No. 2 A letter from Father Julius Jette, Nov. 1902; No. 3. A letter from Father Julius Jette, August 11, 1902
3. Missionary Journeys in Alaska—A letter of Father Philip Delon to Very Rev. Richard A. Gleeson, May 29, 1916. (These letters courtesy of the Reverend Paul O'Connor)

The Voice of Alaska, Sister Mary Joseph Calasanctius
Dogsled Apostles, A. H. Savage
American Baptists in Alaska, pamphlet
The Salvation Army in Alaska, Chester Taylor, unpublished manuscript.

ABOUT THE AUTHOR

Tay Thomas began to write poetry as a child, with her first prose poem published in a New York City newspaper at seventeen. The same young age was true of flying: her family treated small planes like cars. Big planes were considered a second home—naturally when her father was a vice president with Pan American Airways. After graduating from Smith College (where she majored in geography) Tay then married Lowell Thomas Jr., a former Air Force pilot, who already owned a small airplane. Together they roamed the world's out-of-way places for five years, paying for the travel by writing and filming for the National Geographic and a children's television program.

Tay and Lowell moved to Alaska with their two young children in 1960. Following a jointly written book entitled *Flight to Adventure*, Tay wrote two more books on Alaska, *Follow The North Star*, and *Only In Alaska*. *Cry in the Wilderness* came next followed by *My War with Worry* and *An Angel On His Wing* (a biography of the Alaska's Episcopal Diocese's flying Bishop.)

Tay then turned to civic and church activities, which included six years on the Anchorage School Board and the founding of the F.I.S.H. organization, with co-workers from a number of local churches providing transportation, food, and housing for newcomers to a rapidly growing city which had little to offer in the way of public services. F.I.S.H. is still going strong today but offers food only, feeding over two thousand families a year.

Once F.I.S.H. was running well, Tay turned her energies toward her church, St. Mary's Episcopal, where she has been head gardener since 1970.

Tay also served her church by teaching the course, Education For Ministry, a Bible study developed by the Sewanee Church Center. She and Lowell also sing in the choir and are active with their family of two children, five granddaughters, and three great grandchildren.

www.ingramcontent.com/pod-product-compliance
Lightning Source LLC
Chambersburg PA
CBHW050839160426
43192CB00011B/2081